# Emily's Rebellion

A BUSINESS GUIDE TO DESIGNING BETTER
TRANSACTIONAL SERVICES
FOR THE DIGITAL AGE

by Lloyd Robinson
with Graham Wilson

Technics Publications
BASKING RIDGE, NEW JERSEY

2 Lindsley Road, Basking Ridge, NJ 07920 USA
https://www.TechnicsPub.com

Cover design by Lorena Molinari
Edited by Lauren McCafferty

First Edition
First Printing 2019
Copyright © 2019 Lloyd Robinson

ISBN, print ed.      9781634624619
ISBN, Kindle ed.    9781634624626
ISBN, PDF ed.      9781634624640

Library of Congress Control Number: 2018966151

# Contents

Foreword ........................................................................................ 1
Preface .......................................................................................... 5
Acknowledgements...................................................................... 9

**PART I: Transaction Foundations** .................................... 11
**Chapter 1: Introduction** ...................................................... 13
    Designing services for the digital age.............................. 13
    Customer-facing and internal journeys distinct but aligned . 17
    The Requirements Black Hole ......................................... 19
    How Emily's rebellion can become a revolution .................... 23
    Concept map ..................................................................... 28
    Emily's glossary ................................................................ 29

**Chapter 2: Trading Sheep in Sumer** ................................ 33
    Transactions create data ................................................... 34
    Recording nouns .............................................................. 36
    Cuneiform ........................................................................ 37
    Data matters..................................................................... 39
    Data is at the heart of a business .................................... 41
    Six kinds of data .............................................................. 48
    How to tell master data from transaction data ...................... 59
    Launching the payload...................................................... 60
    Managing transaction data better .................................... 62
    Three key points from this chapter.................................. 65
    Further reading................................................................. 66

**Chapter 3: Responding to Requests** ................................ 67
    People, patterns, and prehistory .................................... 67
    Business processes and the transaction pattern ...................... 76
    Transactions comprise a request and a response.................... 77
    Transactions exchange value........................................... 81
    Transacting requires a decision....................................... 83
    Transactions follow a pattern of changing statuses.............. 84
    A generic pattern of request and response ...................... 90

Requests are resilient to changing response processes ........... 91
Varying the transaction pattern .................................................. 92
Three styles of transactional complexity .................................... 95
Three key points from this chapter .......................................... 103

**Chapter 4: Experience the Service ............................................. 105**
The Service Design approach .................................................... 108
A service blueprint sets the context for transaction design .. 120
Identifying transactions ............................................................ 124
Three key points from this chapter .......................................... 133
Further reading ........................................................................... 133

**Chapter 5: Grand Designs ........................................................... 135**
Form and function ...................................................................... 137
Why does business need an architecture? ............................... 142
Business architects understand how the business works ..... 148
How does architecture help Emily? .......................................... 153
Three key points from this chapter .......................................... 161
Further reading ........................................................................... 161

**PART II: Transaction Methods ......................................... 163**
**Chapter 6: A Job to Do ................................................................. 165**
Getting down to work ................................................................ 167
Initiate phase .............................................................................. 170
Submit phase ............................................................................... 173
Validating before processing .................................................... 174
Validate phase ............................................................................. 176
Decide phase ............................................................................... 177
Complete phase .......................................................................... 180
Like transactions, tasks also have a status .............................. 182
The flow of work tasks through the workplace ...................... 184
The data about transactions and tasks can be generalized ... 189
Bringing all these ideas together ............................................. 195
Roles people play ....................................................................... 198
Three key points from this chapter .......................................... 202
Further reading ........................................................................... 203

**Chapter 7: A Task Shared is a Task Halved** ............................ 205
What tasks can be shared across transactions? ...................... 208
Arrange the pattern diagram differently .................................. 209
Shared tasks interlock with transaction-specific tasks .......... 211
Specification of requirements for shared tasks ...................... 215
Identification ................................................................................ 216
Notification tasks ........................................................................ 222
Payment ........................................................................................ 224
Approval ....................................................................................... 225
Future activity scheduling ......................................................... 227
Customer interactions ................................................................. 227
Three key points from this chapter .......................................... 228

**Chapter 8: Interacting with Customers** ................................ 229
Interactions move transactions forward .................................. 230
Categories of interactions ........................................................... 234
Channels for interacting ............................................................. 236
Data about interactions .............................................................. 239
Verbal interactions ...................................................................... 240
Informal written interactions .................................................... 242
Formal written interactions ....................................................... 243
Why is this important? ................................................................ 250
Three key points from this chapter .......................................... 251

**Chapter 9: Do we know what we want?** ................................ 253
A framework for discussing requirements .............................. 254
Getting the workshop underway ............................................... 258
Overview of the transaction ...................................................... 258
Stepping through the five phases ............................................. 259
Wrapping up the workshop ....................................................... 267
Documenting your workshop outputs ..................................... 268
Reviewing a transaction requirements document ................. 280
How is the transaction requirements document used? ......... 282
Three key points from this chapter .......................................... 284

**PART III: Implementing Transactions** ................................. 285
**Chapter 10: Fomenting Revolution** ............................. 287
   Managing change ........................................................ 291
   Managing the change of adopting the Transaction Pattern .. 294
   Transaction Pattern techniques ...................................... 297
   Steps to implementing the Transaction Pattern ............... 300
   Three key points from this chapter ................................. 301
   Further reading ........................................................... 302

**Chapter 11: Putting the Pattern into Practice** ............. 303
   The case study scenario ............................................... 305
   The value stream ......................................................... 306
   The customer journey .................................................. 307
   The business objects and data ...................................... 309
   Narrowing the focus to one transaction ......................... 312
   The business objects in the submit claim transaction ........... 313
   The insurance claim business process ............................. 317
   Align the process to the Transaction Pattern .................. 319
   Eliminate unnecessary business tasks ............................ 320
   Holding a requirements workshop ................................. 324
   Creating the transaction requirements document ............. 326
   Improving the transaction requirements document ........... 330
   Communicating the transaction requirements document .... 331
   Three key points from this chapter ................................. 331

**Chapter 12: Emily's Triumph** ...................................... 333
   A wide range of benefits ............................................... 336
   Benefits in the internal process domain ......................... 337
   Benefits in the data domain .......................................... 344
   Benefits in the customer experience domain ................... 349
   Benefits in the harmonization domain ........................... 351
   The benefits ultimately contribute to strategic outcomes ..... 356
   Three key points from this chapter ................................. 359
   Further reading ........................................................... 360

**Index** ........................................................................ 363

# Foreword

On the first morning of my new job I stepped into the coffee shop and looked around for Lloyd. Lloyd and I have known each other for my entire life, but this was our first time working together, and my first foray into the big unknown (and slightly daunting) world of data management and business architecture. With a background in stakeholder relations, project management, critical thinking and analysis, I'd always stayed firmly on the content side of the business, and never delved into the deep dark basement where the IT section sat. I'd always figured that I didn't need to understand the magic that went on in there, as long as all my systems performed, I could access the data I needed, and I was equipped to assist my clients effectively. When an opportunity arose to work for Lloyd as a liaison between business and IT on a multimillion-dollar project, I was excited by the opportunity to explore a new side of business and gain a better understanding of what goes on behind the scenes.

I found Lloyd sitting in the sunshine, and was introduced to Graham, who immediately pulled out several diagrams he'd tucked under his elbow, ready to go. Together they began to outline the project's progress to date, framed by the theory of transaction patterns, and a description of the transactions relevant to this particular business and its customers. In typical fashion, Lloyd wandered into long and unexpected, yet uniquely enlightening and pertinent analogies, while Graham built from the ground up a clear image of the situation in his trademark measured and illustrative manner. I was hooked from that morning by Lloyd and Graham's passion and vision for their work, and the streamlined methodology which they used to follow through on their ideas. With their remarkable ability to communicate complex concepts to me, a business person with limited experience on IT projects (just like the titular Emily), and their enthusiasm literally shining in their eyes, they had me raring to go within minutes.

Since that day, I have sat in countless meetings where well-intentioned and hard-working employees and managers go around and around in circles, trying to move forward inch by inch on large IT projects, without a guiding philosophy to pull their ideas together and give them a path forward. Perhaps they have created a product that only skims the surface of their customers' needs, or they're facing complex and far-reaching data challenges, but seem capable of processing only smaller issues like deciding the location of a log in button on a webpage. Perhaps each team within the organization has a different business process, and none of them align with one another, let alone with the ideal customer journey. In each of these situations and faced with each of these problems I have felt Emily's need for a rebellion. 'Surely,' I have said to myself, 'there is a better way to create the changes the organization wants, faster and more effectively. Surely, there is a way to ensure organization-wide clear communication, as well to design a business strategy that leads to staff support and engagement, alongside enhanced services. Surely, it is possible to create a methodology that can build upon the knowledge and advances that have already occurred in the industry, while also striking out boldly to overcome existing problems in current methodologies.' In each of these circumstances, Lloyd and Graham have been my daily mentors, guiding me in the direction of real change and business improvement, providing hope, a vision, and most importantly a well-reasoned plan, often while confronted with a group of disillusioned employees and managers who feel lost and despairing aboard a project they don't know how to save from sinking.

This is the gift that *Emily's Rebellion* now offers more broadly to readers everywhere. Here for the first time in writing are the concepts and methods Lloyd and Graham so generously shared with me for all of us to consider, discuss and build upon. This book is a new map of how we can navigate the complex waters of large IT projects and find our way through to the other side with both an effective product and our sanity intact. The projects that we work on have so much potential, and can affect important changes for our businesses, our clients and our community. *Emily's Rebellion* urges us to take the next step – by building on the knowledge developed by skilled IT practitioners and talented business people over the years –

to move forward into a new method of creating change and delivering results.

Together Lloyd and Graham have over 50 years of experience working on large IT projects. The range and depth of their experience in the field, their nuanced and sophisticated interpretation of the industry, and their boundless passion and intellect have put them in the unique position of being able to offer us this leap into the future: a leap that supports customer services, improves the business, and importantly, is achievable and repeatable across projects. And so their book, *Emily's Rebellion*, is a book for the Emily in us all – it is a call to arms for everyone who has ever sat in a meeting and thought there must be a better way, or watched an IT and a business person speaking different languages to one another over and over again, or wondered how they can *just turn this project around*. My hope for *Emily's Rebellion* is that it is picked up by all those across the industry who have felt or can imagine feeling the spark of Emily's rebellion in the air. May they find within this book a seed of inspiration, as well as tools to effect the changes for which they've been hankering. And finally, may *Emily's Rebellion* snowball into a larger revolution, where our industry and IT projects everywhere continue to develop – always discovering and incorporating new ways in which we can move together towards better outcomes and brighter futures.

**Deborah Noble, Business Analyst, Brisbane, 2018**

# Preface

*Emily's Rebellion* presents a new method of removing the complexity from business processes and information systems. The Transaction Pattern applies pattern thinking to designing and specifying transactional processing requirements. The method is especially suitable for digital transformation initiatives.

Our readers are business people, most likely middle managers who have operational responsibilities. We wrote *Emily's Rebellion* for these people, often called 'subject matter experts', who are required to inhabit the space between the everyday operations of their business and technology 'improvement', 'refresh', and 'digital transformation' projects. Too often, we feel, these spaces seem like a war zone, with the business often ending up with little real business improvement, and 'transformation' that exists more in the mind of a leader who wants to be known for keeping up with the latest trends than in reality. IT specialists will also benefit from this book by learning about a method that could improve their ability to work with their business peers and to deliver systems that truly improve the business.

*Emily's Rebellion* will show you how to methodically specify business requirements, work tasks, workflow, and data requirements, using the Transaction Pattern as a framework. In this book, we use the persona 'Emily' to represent any business person (not a computing specialist) who may find involvement in an IT project to be a miserable experience.

Emily is feeling rebellious. A clever 30-something wanting a change, Emily is dismayed that her boss has given her the 'challenge' of being the subject matter expert for a new IT project. Her friends have told her that IT projects always seem to be an exercise in disappointment, frustration, and missed opportunities. Her job is to specify the business requirements for the new system. Emily knows her part of the business well and she can see that there are inefficiencies in the way the team does things now. The system contains dozens of screens used for data-recording, but it is not oriented towards stepping through a transaction from beginning to end. In fact, there is no clear delineation between the different types of transactions that the business deals with.

Emily hasn't been closely involved with an IT project before. She feels intimidated by the IT guys who demand to know her requirements, and talk of 'functional specifications' and 'user stories'. She doesn't understand all their jargon about object orientation, unified modeling, data-driven design, etc. She feels inadequate for not understanding what they are talking about and what they expect from her. The business analysts on the project team confuse her even more by showing her their previous work – one person shows her a document that lists requirement after requirement for a hundred pages and more. Other analysts show her their one-sentence constructions they call 'user stories' which they say the IT guys could use to develop a system function. Writing a few user stories seems like easy work, but Emily is awestruck by the magic that is promised by this new 'agile' approach. Emily can't understand how the IT analysts and developers could ever hope to develop a coherent system that meets all these individual requirements in a joined-up way. There seems to be an unspoken assumption that a new system supporting a better way of doing business will emerge, as if by magic. After all, an improved business operation – not just a new system – is the point of this investment, isn't it?

Business operations revolve around transactions, which all follow a similar path. When a customer chooses to use a service that Emily's business offers, they first submit a request for that service, like a shopping order, or an application for a permit. The business must deal with this request and eventually provide a response back to the customer – the fulfilment of the order, or a decision on granting the permit. Each business exists to process such transactions, no matter what kind of business it is.

Emily begins to think about her business needs using a new structure. It strikes her that most of the transactional processes are quite similar, it is only the content (the data, the workflow, the output) that varies. There are lots of transactions, but one type of transaction goes to one team and another type goes to another team. Data needs to be captured for each transaction but the data for an order, say, is different than the data needed to process a change of address. But every type of transaction has a similar need for data that tracks where the transaction is up to in the business process, who is dealing with it, and so on. Also, the tasks that the staff perform to process a transaction generally include receiving a customer request, validating it, assessing the request, and deciding how to respond, followed by notifying the customer of the response.

Emily thinks that an approach structured around straightforward patterns like these might simplify how she specifies the business requirements. Looking at each business task in turn, she could focus more on the business workflows, data needs, and business rules, and less on system functionality and screens. She would be able to retain a holistic view of how the business could work more smoothly, processing its transactions like a clock ticking over the minutes from one state to another.

But could the IT team consume her new way of specifying requirements? Would her small rebellion succeed?

We offer this book as one solution to help Emily and her colleagues to achieve better outcomes in their IT projects. Walk with Emily through its pages as she discovers a better path.

# Acknowledgements

The authors wish to thank the following for their invaluable assistance and contributions towards bringing *Emily's Rebellion* to fruition.

Our Emily-like colleagues Rosemary Gallaher, Hope McManus, and Deborah Noble provided numerous insightful comments on the coherence of the text for business readers. Their thoughts and impressions led to significant revisions of the manuscript where important concepts lacked clarity. Rosemary, Hope, and Deborah also helped us bring Emily to life on the pages.

Our long-time collaborator Todd Heather, a former government chief technology officer, offered extremely helpful suggestions for improving the chapters on implementing the Transaction Pattern in projects and on the benefits to be gained from using the pattern. Todd led us to see the far-reaching benefits of the Transaction Pattern.

Our test reader Sebastian Harvey offered further helpful suggestions for improving the manuscript in the later stages of development. Thank you, Seb.

Graham gives special thanks to his employer, Robinson Ryan, for the opportunity to devote time to crafting the manuscript and to bring Lloyd's concepts to the page.

Finally, we wish to thank Deborah Noble for her generous foreword. It was a deep pleasure to have Deborah work with us for a time, through which our ideas – and how to explain them – matured greatly.

# PART I

---

# Transaction Foundations

In Part I, Transaction Foundations, we introduce some ideas and concepts that, taken together, will help business folk take a stronger leadership role when handed the responsibility of being the subject matter expert or executive sponsor of a business improvement project. We also present the structure of the Transaction Pattern, which helps to express business requirements in a structured, well-organized manner.

# Transaction Foundations

# CHAPTER 1

# Introduction

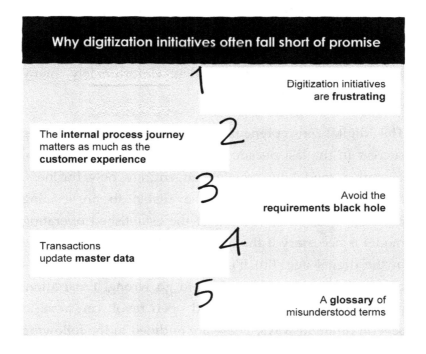

Why digitization initiatives often fall short of promise

1 — Digitization initiatives are **frustrating**

2 — The **internal process journey** matters as much as the **customer experience**

3 — Avoid the **requirements black hole**

4 — Transactions update **master data**

5 — A **glossary** of misunderstood terms

## Designing services for the digital age

Digital services define the age we live in and everyone is doing digital. But digital often falls short of its promise. *Digitization* is the process of using tools and technology to improve business services. Some digitization efforts fail to realize any real improvement in service quality or efficiency. A common mistake is to add a 'digital service' on the front-end of a tired and inefficient internal process – like erecting an enticing new façade in front of an old and decrepit building. A key objective of digitization is improving the customer experience and the journey they take through their interactions with a business. Customer-facing journeys are where many digitization efforts start and place most of their attention. Unfortunately, many digital projects end there as well.

The digital entrepreneurs, who achieved astonishing success in the last decade or so, achieved a new internal operating model by creating an entirely new business. Although this option is not available to an existing business, a major reworking of the established operating model is necessary if the business is to survive and thrive in the digital age. But it's plain hard work, and, what's more, it's very easy for things to go wrong. Frustration, confusion, anger, agitation, and open revolt can arise in several different ways. These are outlined in the following paragraphs.

Your colleagues are weary of the constant change initiatives that do not seem to achieve much. Everyone is aware that the pace of change is accelerating. There are many factors that drive this acceleration, not least technology innovation and constant drives for cost savings. But the cumulative effect of change after change on staff is often great fatigue and – ironically – less efficiency and fleeting benefits. How can we manage change initiatives that really 'stick' and make a lasting difference?

Your staff are tired of the clumsy computer systems that they are forced to use. Most of your staff have joined the workforce since computerized business systems became ubiquitous. They don't remember the card systems and paper-based processes of older times. They do not understand why they can order their groceries online on their smartphones with a few finger presses, yet at work they must use a complicated and unfriendly business system. They must learn from others, or by trial and error, how to *really* use the system. They devise off-system work-arounds and unplanned manual tasks to get their job done. Digitized services will not be successful if you rely on such awkward systems and processes in the back-office.

Your managers are frustrated by the lack of up-to-date information about the state of their team's workload. They are tired of finding out about tasks that have been misplaced or forgotten via a call from an angry customer. They want to know when a task has not been performed to the correct service level *before* the target service level expires, not *afterwards*. They want to know what tasks need to be reprioritized or reallocated because of staff absences, at the start of the day, not at the end. Digitized services need real-time management information.

Your experienced staff, who know and understand the business well, protest about the barriers that IT folk create when new requirements are explored. They struggle when technical jargon is the only language that their IT colleagues can express themselves in. They cannot believe the long delivery lead times, even when the developers use 'agile' methods. And they quickly lose heart when faced with features that are promised but never delivered.

Your board and chief executive baulk at the spiraling cost of computer systems, and repeated failures of IT projects to deliver benefits to the business. In the rapidly changing landscape of digitization and disruptive business models, digital services need to deliver a return on investment quickly. The board must be confident in the ability of digitization to rapidly realize benefits, or further investment funds will not be forthcoming.

From all directions, attempting to digitize your business and overturn your old operating model is a recipe for serious and uncontrollable disaster. To avert disaster, a different approach is needed. The stage is set for a revolution. Leaders who drive successful digitization projects understand that there are, not one, but two aspects to doing digital. Whilst allowing customers to transact with your business digitally is obvious, the second – and equally important – aspect of digitizing a business service is the internal process journey. The responsiveness and quality of your operational processes in the back-office should mirror the expectations raised by the improvements to the customer-facing journey. They are two sides of the same coin. A recent report emphasized the potential benefits resulting from considering both aspects of digitization:

> *Digital tools have the capacity to transform customer-facing journeys in powerful ways, often by creating the potential for self-service. Digital can also reshape time-consuming transactional and manual tasks that are part of internal journeys, especially when multiple systems are involved.* [1]

---

## The customer-facing and internal process journeys are distinct but aligned

The alignment between the customer-facing journey and the internal process journey is illustrated in Figure 1-1:

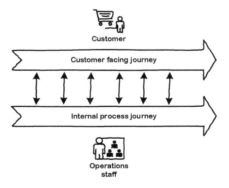

Figure 1-1 Customer journey and internal process journey are aligned

---

[1] McKinsey & Company https://mck.co/2kp2gUQ.

Figure 1-2 shows a simple example, of applying for a driver license, illustrating how the customer-facing journey must align to the internal process journey. For most of the activities within the customer-facing journey there is a corresponding activity in the internal processes within the driver licensing authority.

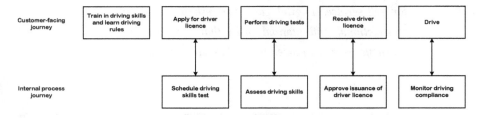

Figure 1-2 Alignment of journeys in driver licensing

A new self-service customer journey should improve the customer's experience and efficiency. However, if the journey takes your staff through time-consuming internal processes, this will limit the efficiency within your operations, raise the level of frustration and boredom of your long-suffering staff, and ultimately affect their level of engagement.

If your goal is to create an excellent digital service, the tasks that operational staff perform every day must also be redesigned. This deserves at least as much care and effort as redesigning the customer-facing journey. By attending to both these aspects of digital service delivery, you will create a 'win-win' outcome for the business as well as for the customer.

In summary, offering a 'digital service' to your customers is not merely putting your front counter onto your customer's computer at home. Delivering service in the digital age requires a new operating model inside the business as well.

## The Requirements Black Hole

The fashions in computer system development circles swing between methods that we can describe generally as 'requirements up-front' and 'requirements as-we-go'. Both approaches have their merits – but likewise, both have their dangers.

In the early days of computing, systems analysts needed to know "what the users want" in great detail – enabling specification of every business rule, data item, and process step – before any build work was done on the computer system. This 'requirements up-front' method came to be referred to as a 'waterfall approach', in which each step of the method, when completed, flowed irreversibly to the next step, like water in a waterfall.

Many failures of 'requirements up-front' IT projects eventually led to the advent of Agile development methods, in which business and IT worked more closely and iteratively, building a component of software quickly, allowing the business to add or change requirements at relatively low cost. The idea of Agile development is that a one-sentence user story is enough to get the software developers going on something. The rest of the requirements emerge during continuous engagement with a business expert and iterative refinement of the software. That is, the industry swung towards building software without knowing very much at all about the business needs at first, in a 'requirements as-we-go' approach. Agile development was revolutionary and is still widely used today, often very successfully when done well.

Both extremes of fashion lead us dangerously close to the irresistible forces of a requirements black hole. The 'requirements up-front' approach encourages never-ending analysis of requirements. In the meantime, business people tend to focus on the faults of the current system – often relatively trivial defects – because these are the things that cause them pain. Consequently, they find it difficult to imagine an entirely different system that will properly support a more efficient way of processing work. The IT experts complain that the business cannot make up its mind.

On the other hand, the 'requirements as-we-go' approach leads to an impatient, "are we there yet?" mindset. That is, multiple cycles of building enough requirements into the software to ensure we can show progress and quickly release something that *works*. At some point, the software is declared to be a 'minimum viable product' suitable for testing by real users, which we refer to as *beta testing*.

Unfortunately, beta testing does not place focus on the everyday usage of the software in a business context; as such, undiscovered requirements will emerge late in the project. Meanwhile, the management pressure to 'go live' increases as time and money run out.

A problem with the 'requirements as-we-go' approach is that it is difficult to know whether the team has delivered a complete, coherent product from all the disparate pieces they have built. The software lacks architecture. It resembles a shanty town more than a structurally sound building. The 'requirements as-we-go' approach is akin to building the foyer of an office block with only a vague concept of the rest of the building.

A solid understanding of the future business journeys, and how they will operate in day-to-day reality, rarely emerges from these contrasting approaches. Neither the voluminous but impractical demands of the 'requirements up-front' approach nor the atomized user stories and working software fragments of 'requirements as-we-go' approach quite fit the bill. What ties these requirements together and ensures that they conform to the business strategy?

Lately, the fashion has swung towards incorporating 'design thinking' and user research into the 'Agile' method. This approach gives us an important perspective on the journey of the customer and enables us to recognize that we must deliver a transactional experience for the customer that completes the journey coherently. This is a refreshing change from the inward-looking focus of previous methodologies. At last we are placing importance on the front-office and facilitating the best approach for the customer.

However, design thinking focuses on the touchpoints or interactions between the customer and the business. There is less emphasis on the full intent of the business and how the internal business processes should be organized to operate efficiently. This is a back-office concern: the internal process journey that should mirror the customer-facing journey, as discussed earlier.

The internal process journey is not as readily designed as the customer interactions – there are a great many factors to consider and bring into balance. What data do we need in the back-office to process this transaction? What are the minimal process tasks required to fulfil the customer's request? How can we apply what we know about one type of transaction to another transaction? How will the team manager know how much work is building up, how many transactions are waiting to be processed? How do we know which team is causing blockages in the business's throughput?

One important factor that helps to clarify our thinking when defining business requirements is that *transactions result in a change to the business's master data*. An order is fulfilled; an account is opened or closed; an invoice is sent;

a payment is received. These activities are recorded in our data. The change that a transaction causes to the master data is what is most important and enduring – it creates a record of the activities of our business. The processes by which these master data records are created and updated are of less long-term significance than the records themselves.

There are recurring patterns to the business activities that process the transactions. If we think about transactional business processes as patterns of business activities that update master data, we open our minds to a different way of defining requirements.

Keeping a project in the safe zone, away from the dangers of the requirements black hole, *can* be done. It requires good management, good design, and active engagement with both the customer journey and the internal process journey. And Emily's fresh perspective on the internal journey is the key.

## How Emily's rebellion can become a revolution

There is comfort in walking a well-trodden path – you know that others have walked that way, and you know that it leads to somewhere good. Ancient walking paths crisscross landscapes where people have travelled for centuries. However, new obstacles, like fallen trees and landslips, can make it necessary to divert off the old path and forge a new track, maybe through unfamiliar country. A new village arises, and we need to make a more direct path to connect it to other places where people live. Sometimes people have made several paths over a landscape and it is not clear which way is best to get to your destination. Such disruptions and alternative pathways are happening to businesses with increasing frequency these days. The old ways are changing rapidly. The old ways of designing and building business systems are now not as useful as they once were, or they don't take you to the correct destination. Emily is keen to understand which development path is the best, the fastest, the most sustainable?

This book provides a guide for business people like Emily to engage in a new revolution. Our guide will help you to think about your business in a different way. It will teach you to *design* your business's services in some detail, and not to leave design to the business process and IT experts. You will understand and be able to communicate why the front-office experience of your customer journey must be supported and counterbalanced by the experience of your process journey in the back-office.

This book will reveal how all your business services conform to a common pattern. Although it doesn't seem so at first glance, your online customer performs a similar sequence of steps, no matter whether they are placing an order, applying for a driver's license, or updating their address. The generic pattern in these different transactions goes like this: they discover the thing they want, enter the information needed, submit it, and receive an acknowledgement.

Similarly, you will see that the internal process journeys follow a similar pattern. Your operators receive and validate the information from the customer, evaluate this information, make a decision about the request, and notify the customer of the outcome. Although the content, business rules, and outputs are different for each journey, many business operations follow this pattern, whether it is fulfilling an order, or deciding whether someone is fit and proper to drive a motor vehicle.

The design method presented in this book will help you to leverage these common patterns to design successful digital services. *Emily's Rebellion* will equip you with a method for defining business requirements for both the front-office and the back-office facets of a service. Our design method is particularly applicable to the design of digital services when complemented by a customer journey design or service design approach. The pattern-based structure will make services easier to design, communicate, and implement. Your customer-facing and internal process journeys will work together seamlessly.

Utilizing this pattern, you will be able to design the structures of your transactional services rapidly and comprehensively. This pattern-based perspective will equip you with the tools to express how you want digitized business processes and customer-facing journeys to be structured.

These tools will release you from dependence on IT professionals to help you with the design of your digital services. Our approach will enable you to take control of digital initiatives, rather than allowing them to be led by IT experts. Despite the term 'digital', doing digital services well is fundamentally not a technology problem. As in the 20th Century Modernist way of thinking about the architecture of buildings, form follows function in computer systems. The intended function of a building is a significant determinant of its shape and size. The form of your computer system is determined by the function that *you* decide it needs to perform. That function is, in turn, determined by the design of the business service that the system is to support.

We will cover the following topics:

- How do customer journeys comprise of individual transactional and information services, and how do I identify them?

- Why do transactional services conform to universally applicable patterns of business tasks that are performed during the processing of a transaction? How does this lead to an implementable workflow?

- How do I use the Transaction Pattern to discover business requirements (e.g. data, rules, routing) quickly and collaboratively?

- Why do transactions always change the data records of my business (i.e. the master data)? How should I store the data about transactions separately to the master data?

- How does using common pattern-based transactions help my business to centralize the management information needed by operations managers to run our internal process journeys smoothly?

- How do I ensure that some business tasks (such as tasks for approval, notification, and identification of the customer) are designed and built once, so that they are reusable across multiple transactions?

- How should I document the design of a transactional service using a pattern?

- How do I help the computer system designers to understand how to implement a pattern-based transaction?

With this knowledge at your disposal, you and other revolutionaries in your business will soon be creating digital services that everyone – your customers as well as your internal processing staff – will love.

## Concept map

Figure 1-3 provides a map of the concepts covered by *Emily's Rebellion* and shows how the concepts are related. Readers could use this map to see at a glance how a particular topic under discussion fits within the overall picture.

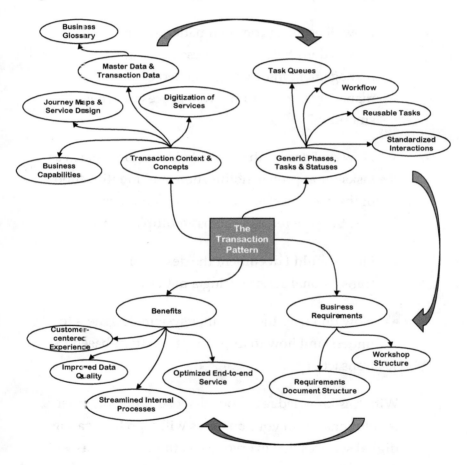

Figure 1-3 Concept Map of the topics covered in *Emily's Rebellion*

# Emily's glossary

Emily quickly finds that people throw terms into their conversations without really knowing what the terms mean. Business words and phrases are easily misunderstood and then reused by someone else but with a slightly different meaning based on what they understood the term to mean. Pretty soon everyone is using the term, but it now has several meanings.

Emily hears several terms of which she does not have a clear understanding. What is a transaction? An interaction? What is a data model? What is workflow? Emily needs some clear definitions so that she can make good use of these terms. Here are her definitions of the key terms used in this book.

Table 1-1 Emily's glossary

| Term | Meaning |
|---|---|
| **Business architecture** | A blueprint (i.e. an abstract representation) of a business that provides a common understanding of the organization. It is used to align strategic objectives and tactical demands, particularly for translating strategy into actionable initiatives. |
| **Business capability** | An ability to do something – a combination of skilled people, business processes, data and information, and technology. How well a business unit does something points to possible improvements that could be made in skills, processes, databases, and systems. |

| Term | Meaning |
|---|---|
| **Business function** | An operating responsibility of an organizational unit; e.g. Unit A performs the Accounts Receivable function – they would undertake many of the tasks in a Billing business process. |
| **Business glossary** | A single, centralized resource about the language used by the organization. The glossary is authoritative, as it has been endorsed and approved by management, and it promotes trust and transparency about the organization's information assets. |
| **Business process** | A sequence of activities or tasks that realize a business objective, such as the delivery of a service to a customer. |
| **Business service** | Businesses exist to provide services to stakeholders, either consumers or other businesses. A business service puts a name to one of those services. Business services are sometimes packaged as products, either physical (cars) or virtual (banking products). There are two types: transactional and information. |
| **Customer journey** | A map expressing a typical customer's perspective of their experience of a service, including the touchpoints where the customer and the business interact and transact. An analysis of a current state customer journey leads to insights about how the customer's experience might be improved. |
| **Customer-facing journey** | Synonym of Customer journey. |

| Term | Meaning |
|---|---|
| **Data model** | A map of the things that the business holds data about; it shows how these things relate to each other. Guides the design of databases so that data is placed in a sound structure that enables consistent storage and retrieval of data. |
| **Information service** | A business service that comprises a one-way exchange of information – e.g. discovery of information on a website, or the balance of a bank account. |
| **Interaction** | An event in which the stakeholders of a business service interact with each other, e.g. to clarify information or send a notification. |
| **Service blueprint** | Documentation of a service design, usually in the form of a map based on the target customer journey. May include customer profiles, service scenarios, cross-channel views, and organizational impact analysis. |
| **Service design** | The skills and tools that facilitate the intentional design of a customer's experience of a service. |
| **Task** | An atomic piece of work – a task can be undertaken in its entirety by one person. |
| **Task queue** | A list of uncompleted tasks that a business stakeholder team or individual needs to undertake – a mechanism for the orderly sequencing of work. A task queue is often ordered 'first-in-first-out' but the priority of a task may be adjusted according to changing circumstances. |
| **Transaction** | A specific exchange of value between two stakeholders, usually a business and a customer. |

| Term | Meaning |
|---|---|
| **Transaction Pattern** | A generic combination of work tasks, grouped into phases, by which a transaction is initiated and processed. |
| **Transactional service** | A reciprocal exchange in which a mutually beneficial transaction occurs. |
| **Value stream** | A high-level business process map showing 5-7 key activities that deliver value to customers; it communicates what the organization is in the business of doing. |
| **Workflow** | The movement of work tasks from one business person, team, or technology system to another. |

# CHAPTER 2

# Trading Sheep in Sumer

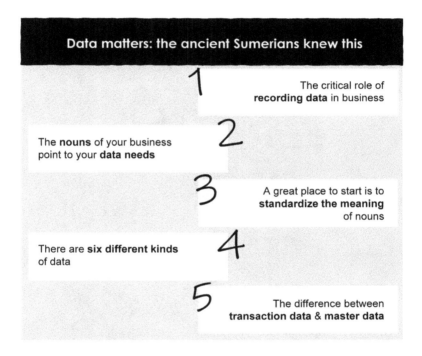

Data matters: the ancient Sumerians knew this

1 The critical role of **recording data** in business

2 The **nouns** of your business point to your **data needs**

3 A great place to start is to **standardize the meaning** of nouns

4 There are **six different kinds** of data

5 The difference between **transaction data** & **master data**

Emily is confused. She knows that the systems she uses every day exist to 'capture' data, but why? What is this wild beast that needs to be captured? Why are the data entry screens filled with so many data fields, and is all of it necessary? Does anyone use it? For what purpose? Is some data more important than other data?

## Transactions create data

At the heart of every transaction lies data that needs to be managed. Transactions cause the updating of data of some sort or another. In this chapter we explain why it is vital to be aware of the data involved in a transaction and to manage that data appropriately.

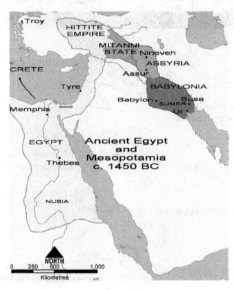

Figure 2-1 A map of the ancient Middle East showing Sumer [2]

The farmers of ancient Sumer understood data. 10,000 years ago, when agriculture developed, Sumerian farmers needed a way to record their animals and goods. A plainly shaped clay token was developed to represent an animal or a container of grain.

---

[2] Public Domain. https://bit.ly/2ScxGKa.

Around 6,000 years ago, clay tokens became more sophisticated and varied in shape. As the production of goods increased, their exchange became more commonplace, and a more efficient way of recording exchanges was necessary. Traders began to place several tokens within a baked clay envelope called a 'bulla'. Impressions were made on the outside of the bulla so that people knew what was inside.

Figure 2-2 Sumerian bulla and contents[3]

Embossed seals represented the parties to the transaction. A bulla had to be broken to alter the information inside, and so, an intact bulla held irrefutable evidence of the facts of a transaction should a dispute arise. Thus, the information contained in a bulla was a permanent record

---

[3] © Marie-Lan Nguyen / Wikimedia Commons / CC-BY 2.5 (https://bit.ly/2r3q94Q), Accountancy clay envelope Louvre Sb1932",https://bit.ly/2m8wXNA.

of a transaction of goods between parties. To Sumerian traders, data mattered.

---

## Recording nouns

These ancient transactional records consisted of tokens that represented a thing – that is, the tokens were like nouns, the names of things. Over time, tokens representing counts of things were developed to reduce the need to make an individual token for each separate thing. With this development, the transaction for a trade of five sheep, for example, could now be represented by only two tokens rather than the five tokens previously needed – one token was required for the noun 'sheep' and one for the count of five, thus making a complete noun + numeral phrase.

In this way, the concept of data was born. Nothing much has changed – today we continue to record transactions using nouns and counts.

There are no verbs in this accounting 'language' and so the Sumerian bulla left no record of the processes the traders used to conduct their exchanges. We may lament this absence that so limits our understanding of the Sumerian trading culture; however, it is likely that trading involved only a few simple actions or processes – handing over the tokens in exchange for goods, storing the tokens inside a bulla, handing the bulla to a third party as security, and, potentially, breaking open the bulla.

Even today, our smartphones contain mostly nouns – 'Contacts' and 'Photos', for example. Actions such as turning, touching, and swiping are the processes of the phone but are not stored as data like contacts and photos. Yet using these simple actions that humans have always been able to perform, we can turn over the phone to accept a call, touch another phone and exchange contacts, swipe and delete an email. Despite their staggering technical complexity under the covers, the universal ability to use a modern phone mimics the simplicity of these early recording systems, with a series of verbs or actions that are used to process nouns or data.

## Cuneiform

Records of transactions evolved into larger clay tablets inscribed with pictograms in the shape of the earlier tokens. Clay tablets rapidly replaced tokens and bulla, as tablets were much cheaper to make. Over subsequent millennia, we have developed ever more efficient methods of recording data about transactions, culminating of course in modern-day digital data.

Around 3700 BC, Sumerian people discovered that pictograms could represent sounds as well as objects or things. This significant advance, known as the Rebus Principle, enabled people to record words that were difficult to represent as pictures. Suddenly it became possible to record verbs.

By about 2500 BC, pictograms became more abstract in the form of simple wedge-shaped marks arranged in patterns. This script, known as cuneiform, was simpler and cheaper than pictograms for recording transactions as it required less space and therefore fewer materials. Over the next few centuries, writing complex sentences became possible using cuneiform – even stories and poetry began to be recorded.

Figure 2-3 Cuneiform tablet[4]

Cuneiform script was so useful that it was adopted by multiple cultures and languages in the Middle and Near East, and used for two and a half thousand years until the first century AD. The famous Rosetta Stone, dated at 500

---

[4] © Marie-Lan Nguyen / Wikimedia Commons https://bit.ly/2P0Z2B2.

BC, relates a story in three languages, all written using cuneiform script. Despite its continuous use over such a long time, cuneiform script retained its patterns of simple wedge-shaped impressions, and is remarkably reminiscent of the ones and zeros of digital data.

## Data matters

As the ancient Sumerians knew, data matters far more than the processes that created it. Data ends up in a business's financial statements, its annual reports, and its communications with customers and other stakeholders. Data fuels management decisions, both strategic and operational. Data is the critical asset that remembers your customers, your product catalogue, your financial accounts, and so on. That is, your data remembers your business.

Whether it is stored in Sumerian clay tokens, bulla, tablets, ledger books, or computer databases, data is created by transactions between stakeholders. In other words, business transactions generate the data that later can be recalled and used, not only as proof of past dealings, but also for many additional purposes, such as to summarize the last month's or year's transactions, to produce 'how are we doing' reports, and to provide the raw material for the business's tax returns.

When a customer transacts with a business, a small shift occurs in the state of the business. An exchange of information occurs – also, perhaps, money and/or goods exchange hands. This shift in the business's state is recorded in the business's data. When a new customer opens a bank account, a new customer record and account record are added to the bank's data. When the customer moves to a new house and notifies their bank, the address on the record for the customer is updated so that the customer's account statements will be sent to the correct address.

Computer systems were primarily designed to manage these data changes. In the early days of using computers to make businesses more efficient, they were known as 'electronic data processing systems'. Systems were used for processing orders, processing sales, processing employees' pay, and processing invoices. The term 'data processing' was – and still is – appropriate for such systems because this is essentially what computerized business systems do – they process changes to data.

As we have seen so far in this chapter, from ancient Sumer to the present day, there is nothing new about the need to record and process data. Businesses have always needed to update their records when a transaction occurs. For centuries, clay tablets and pen-and-paper provided the technology to do this important task. Data processing systems simply turned pen-and-paper ledger books, order books, and card-based stock inventories into digital bits and bytes. In the next section, we look at the different kinds of data that are managed by computers today.

## Data is at the heart of a business

Data is represented in the nouns of your business. You will discover references to these data 'nouns' not only in data models, but throughout documents containing business processes and procedures, reports and statistics, functional structure and job titles, business systems and applications. We can refer to these nouns as 'data subjects', meaning the things that we keep data about.

For example, a business process named 'Customer pays premium for insurance policy' contains three nouns – customer, premium, and policy. (Note that insurance is a noun too, but it is special because it is behaving like an adjective, signifying a type of policy.) These nouns reflect the data that is involved in the business process, because when an insurance premium is paid, a record needs to be made of the payment, who made it, and for what purpose. That is, the premium payment data is linked to a customer record and to a policy record. Identifying the data subjects in your business is a matter of looking for the nouns.

Of course, most businesses use different words to mean the same thing – customer, client, stakeholder, buyer, purchaser, participant, etc. A wise business will define these terms carefully, including any allowed synonyms, and encourage consistent use of the terms. Many terms have clear-cut meanings, but others will always be problematic.

Take 'student', for example, a term that pervades the education industry. 'Student' can mean many different things depending on your point of view or role in the industry. To an admissions officer, 'student' may be a person who has been admitted to a course of study; to a teacher, 'student' may be a person who is enrolled in a unit they are teaching in the current semester; to an administrator, 'student' may be any person who has ever enrolled whether studying now or not; to the alumni association, 'student' means someone who has graduated and completed a course of study; to the marketing department, 'student' could be a person who is considering studying; and so on. This situation is fertile ground for confusion and misunderstanding.

To illustrate how confusing this can get, let's look at the contrast between two versions of the same diagram. The first, shown in Figure 2-4, is the anarchic result of business silos using their own terms and working in isolation. Different nouns are used for the same real-world thing. The second diagram (Figure 2-5), in which common terms are used, shows a much more joined-together business that has a better prospect of delivering consistent services to students. A standardized definition of a term enables it to be used for many different purposes. As shown in Figure

2-5, the standardized term 'Student' is used in the college's statement of its business objectives, the names of its services, its business processes, and the subject areas that it holds information about. This is especially valuable in the case of business design documentation, such as process maps, procedures, customer journey maps, and information models.

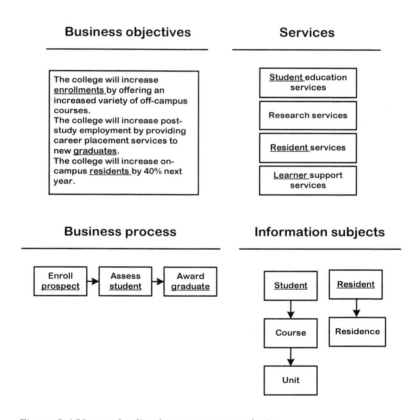

Figure 2-4 Unstandardized terms cause confusion

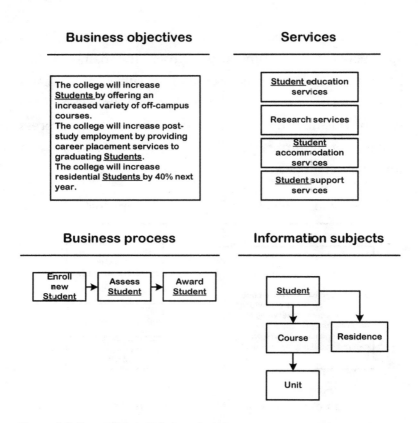

Figure 2-5 Common terms bring clarity

Just as the architect of a building will communicate both with their client and with the engineer and builder using standardized language (everyone knows what 'door' or 'beam' means), a business architect or service designer uses the defined nouns throughout documents and diagrams that present views of the business. The nouns are defined in a business glossary, a data dictionary, or a high-level data model. Each noun will almost invariably relate to a category of data that is captured and used by the business.

## Business Glossary

A single, centralized resource about the language used by the organization. The glossary is authoritative, as it has been endorsed and approved by management, and it promotes trust and transparency about the organization's information assets.

The value of a business glossary has many facets, some of which are:

- Greater alignment across organizational units by disambiguating terms;
- Better decision making by shifting the burden from defining problems, to solving them;
- Easier policy implementation by having a centralized repository of policy terms, precisely identifying their sources;
- Greater awareness & transparency of data assets & business processes;
- Greater regulatory compliance by promoting engagement and awareness of the policies, laws, rules, and reporting requirements.

There is even a problem with using the term 'student'. 'Student' is a perfectly legitimate unifying concept to use when describing the business situation of an educational institution (and certainly far better than using a mixture of 'student', 'learner', 'prospect', 'graduate', and 'resident'). When it comes to designing and building information systems, however, there is a need for greater precision in our use of terms. A person is admitted to a course of study – this makes them a student. The person and the student are the same thing. If they withdraw from the course, they are no longer a current student – but the person still exists. Their historic admission to the course is knowledge that we don't want to lose. Therefore, 'student' is actually a term for the *relationship* between a person and a course.

So, the only nouns we need when describing the data are Person and Course – 'student' is superfluous. Person and Course are much easier to define clearly – that is, Person and Course are stable and distinct real-world concepts. As we saw above, student is not a stable concept. And since it is so ambiguous and unnecessary, 'student' can be eliminated entirely.

Therefore 'student' is not a data subject, it expresses a type of a relationship a person has with another data subject – actually, several relationships (which is why it is such an ambiguous term). The student relationships may include:

- Person is admitted to Course;
- Person is enrolled in Unit;
- Person lodges in Residence;
- Person has Assessment for Unit;
- Person is awarded Qualification;
- Person is granted Scholarship.

The capitalized nouns in the above list are all data subjects, also known as data concepts or business objects. We can draw a simple map of the data subjects outlined in the above list of relationships, as shown in Figure 2-6. This type of diagram is called a 'data model' – it models some or all of the relevant data subjects, the nouns of the business.

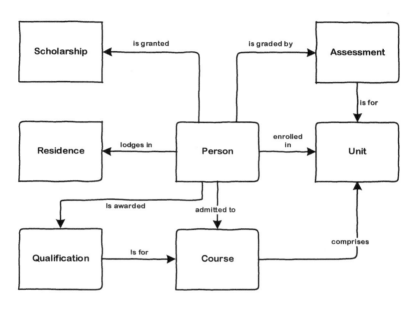

Figure 2-6 Data concepts for an educational institute (partial)

There are many more relationships that a person may have with other education-related subjects, such as a teacher of a unit, as an administrator, and as a prospect for a course of study. A person can – all at the same time – be admitted to a course, be enrolled in units, have already been awarded a qualification, be employed by the university as a tutor, and have a scholarship. All these roles are simply relationships between the person and other subjects. The word 'student' is not necessary to describe these data subjects and relationships.

So, should the word 'student' be eliminated from our vocabulary? Good luck with that. 'Student' is such a widespread term that it will survive no matter what data specialists think about it. However, this discussion is not suggesting the word needs to be excised from the language; our opinion is that 'student' is not precise enough a term to use in relation to data about students. It is good data design to excise 'student' from the model of the organization's data. Nevertheless, it remains a useful word – a kind of shorthand for 'a person who is enrolled, or has ever been enrolled, in a course'. As this example shows, data can get complicated very quickly, but we can keep control of the complexity by doing two things:

- clearly defining our nouns, and
- distinguishing nouns that are placeholders for a relationship between data subjects.

It takes time and experience to analyze your business's data subjects skillfully, so seek the assistance of an experienced data modeler.

## Six kinds of data

All data is not created equal. Some data forms the most important records of a business – we term this type of data 'master data'. Master data is the precious payload of our transactions. However, the payload is but a fraction of the data that a business operation needs to process the transaction, and others like it, smoothly and efficiently.

As the transaction is initiated and progresses through submission and decision-making steps, data is created so that operational staff can monitor the transaction's progress. This kind of data is termed 'transaction data'. The accumulating transaction data informs staff what work needs to be done next. With good quality transaction data at hand, a manager can control their team's workload and rebalance the workload when staff are absent.

These two types of data – master data and transaction data – are the bread-and-butter of computerized business systems, ever since they came into the commercial business world as 'electronic data processing' machines. In addition, there are four other types of data, illustrated in Figure 2-7 below. The diagram shows six types of data in all. Each type of data has a different purpose; therefore each type has either more or less strategic importance. Increasingly, computer systems store all types of data, but this was not always the case.

The lower layers of Figure 2-7 – transaction data and audit data – form the more mundane data that records the business's day-to-day operations. Transaction data is critical on the day it is created and immediately afterwards, but quickly loses its usefulness. Transaction data is commonly aggregated to produce statistics on operational throughput and service level achievement.

Once aggregated in this way, data about transactions has little enduring value beyond resolving specific issues that may arise with specific transactions. In contrast, the master data that is created or changed by transactions is of significant enduring interest to the business.

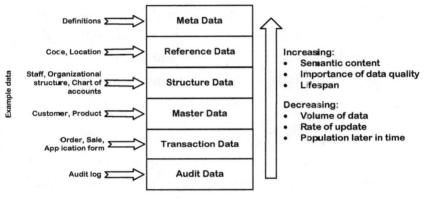

Figure 2-7 The Six Kinds of Data[5]

For an online retailer or a wholesaler, it is critical to the business's survival that a customer's order is processed and fulfilled quickly, without losing the information about what the customer purchased. The correct price needs to be charged and the inventory needs to be updated so that a replacement product can be ordered when the stock level reaches the minimum – this is master data. A year later, there is little value to the business in recalling the details about how they processed that sale, or perhaps even which salesperson made the sale – this is transaction data.

---

[5] After Chisholm, Malcolm (2008). "What is master data?" https://bit.ly/22q7vzi.

The layers in the middle of Figure 2-7 comprise data that has a longer life because the data is about the structure of the business, who the customers are and what products and services the business offers. These are the master data and structure data layers. Structure data holds information about the structure of the business itself, while master data holds the critical records of the outside world and its current relationship with the business.

---

**The Six Kinds of Data**

Metadata – defines the meaning of the nouns that we use in systems and processes, the 'data dictionary'.

Reference data – things that you 'look up', such as lists of countries, list of permitted values.

Structure data – information about the structure of the business itself.

Master data – data about the outside world and its current relationship with the business.

Transaction data – data that records the business's day-to-day operations.

Audit data – detailed information captured when an action occurs in a system.

---

The day-to-day activities of the business are captured in the transaction data layer. These activities cause changes to occur in the records held in the master data layer. For example, when a customer notifies the business that they have moved, the business updates the address held on the customer's master record. When a product sale occurs, the business will adjust the stock inventory master record and create an invoice master record.

The lowest data layer is audit data, which is detailed information captured when an action occurs in a system. Audit data is created by business systems in large log files. We do not need to examine audit data very often; we should be thankful for that, because it is very difficult to interpret as it is stored in a compressed technical format. Audit data becomes useful, however, when a technical defect needs to be traced to its source, or when the user who performed an action needs to be identified. The latter is particularly important when evidence must be produced in the case of a dispute with a customer or regulatory authority.

The highest layers of Figure 2-7 are reference data and metadata. Reference data comprises things that you 'look up', such as lists of countries, list of permitted values of certain data fields (the allowed values that describe a person's gender, to take a common example), datasets of all the physical addresses in a country. Most businesses have many such reference data lists and sets. By centralizing these reference lists, we raise our data quality by ensuring that the same set of values constrains all occurrences of a data item.

The top layer is metadata. Commonly described as 'data about data', metadata defines the meaning of the nouns that we use in our systems and processes. Accordingly, metadata is often called the 'data dictionary'. Well-documented and universally applied metadata ensures that staff can readily discover the meaning and proper usage of any data item in the business's databases.

The differences between the six kinds of data can be difficult to grasp at first – an illustrative example may help your understanding.

When a new driver applies for a license, they must pass all the prescribed tests. When the test results satisfy the criteria, the motor registry must approve a new license to be issued. The registry creates an enduring record of the license that can be retrieved when needed any time in the future. A few years later, the license record is critical to ensuring that infringements of traffic law can be enforced effectively. Also, the license record is useful for demanding a new license fee when the expiration date is reached. Therefore, the license is master data, having a long life. But at the time of a traffic offence or license renewal, it is much less likely that the registry would want to recall who the testing officer was, the date and place of the test, or what the initial license fee was. The data that concerns the license application process is transaction data, not master data.

While the transaction of granting a driver's license is in progress, the motor registry needs to keep track of the driver's application and the many tasks involved in receiving, qualifying, testing, approving, issuing, and recording the license. They do this by creating data about the transaction, and then using that data to manage and monitor the operational processing of the license application transaction. So, transaction data has a very important role to play, even though its relevance is short-lived compared to master data.

The motor registry stores **master data** about the actual licenses they have issued to drivers, while a new driver's application for a license creates **transaction data**. A license application transaction creates a new driver master record and a newly issued license record. When the transaction has been completed (that is, once the driver has been tested and approved), the transaction data holds links to the new master data about the driver and the issued license. This is illustrated in Figure 2-8.

The transaction data also holds the type of license that the driver applied for (e.g., car, motorcycle, or truck). Separately, the motor registry stores a complete and definitive list of the types of driver licenses it offers – this list is **reference data**. The reference list of all types of licenses that can be granted to drivers is very stable over long periods of time. In fact, the kinds of driver licenses are usually enshrined in the government legislation that authorized the registrar to issue licenses. If the legislation is amended to remove or add a new license type, then the reference data must be updated so it continues to match the legislation.

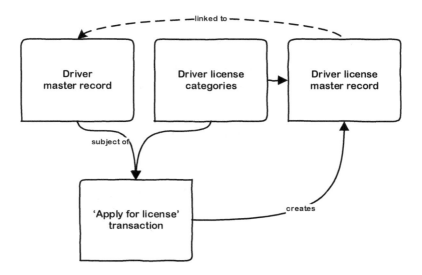

Figure 2-8 A successful license application creates a license master record and a driver master record

The master data for drivers and issued licenses are kept separate because they relate to two distinct objects – a driver and a license. The importance of this separation becomes clear when you consider that a driver may hold more than one class of license – if they drive a car and a truck, for example. If the driver's details are mixed in with the license information, then when the second license is issued the driver's details would be duplicated in two license master records. This makes it more difficult to update the driver's details when they change their name or address. Inevitably, this leads to poor quality data that will come back to haunt the registry at some point, such as during enforcement of driving infringements.

When the driver license expires, a new transaction occurs, involving the payment of a renewal fee and a vision test. The driver license master record is updated with the new expiration date, a new photo of the driver, and any change to the driver's address or name. This data is printed onto a fresh license card, which is given to the driver. The relationships between the master records and the renewal transaction are shown in Figure 2-9.

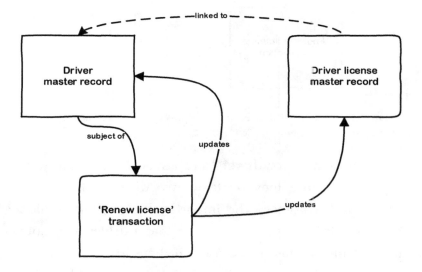

Figure 2-9 Renewing a license updates the license master

The details about the renewal transaction lose their importance once the payment has been processed and the master record has been updated. Of course, the business may choose to keep it for a few weeks or months in case there are any problems, or for management reporting purposes. But the value of the transaction data diminishes rapidly. However, it is critical that the registry retains the updated license master record, or they – and the police – will not be able to do their jobs in enforcing road laws.

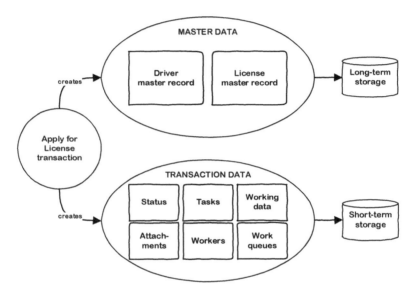

Figure 2-10 Maintaining usefulness

As shown in Figure 2-10, master data and transaction data remain useful for different timespans. Due to the differing longevity of the data, master data has different management needs to the data about transactions. Master data forms the heart of the business – it holds critical and enduring information about our products, customers, customer accounts, etc. On the other hand, data about transactions is critical whilst the transaction is in progress, but quickly fades in significance once the transaction has completed. We do not need to hang onto it forever.

Since our uses for master data and for transaction data are fundamentally different, they can be separated in our databases and managed differently. Nevertheless, there is benefit to be gained from unifying the way in which we manage transaction data across all the transactional services.

So far, of the six layers of data, this example has covered three: **master data**, **transaction data**, and **reference data**. Now we will look at the remaining three layers, **structure data**, **metadata**, and **audit data**.

The registry's organizational structure shows the team structures and supervisory reporting lines. This is structure data. **Structure data** holds information about the business itself. As the name suggests, structure data is structural rather than transactional. For example, storing data about the organizational structure enables the registry's managers to report the performance of the teams for which they are responsible. Performance data from individual teams can be aggregated at the different levels represented by the organizational structure. If there were three teams of driver testers, for example, each tester will belong to one of the teams in the organizational structure. The performance of the three teams can be compared.

The uppermost layer – **metadata** – defines the meaning of objects such as 'driver' and 'license'. The metadata for these objects also stores information about the attributes of the object, such as 'name' and 'address' for the 'driver' object. These definitions help to govern the organization's data assets by providing a framework to guide what data may be stored in which objects. Having a dictionary or business glossary of well-defined data objects is the first step towards improving and maintaining data quality.

The final data layer is **audit data**, which is a log of actions that occur in a system. The kinds of actions that are captured in audit data might include when a driver master record is updated, for example. The audit log will retain a snapshot of the old record before it was amended, or at least of the individual data fields that were changed. If the driver's surname was changed, then the audit log would capture the old and new values of the surname, the user who changed it, and the date and time it was changed. The driver licensing example is summarized in Figure 2-11.

---

## How to tell master data from transaction data

This book is focused on transactions and the effect that transactions have on master data. So, of the six kinds of data, we are mainly interested in the master data and transaction data layers. How do we distinguish between master data and data about the transactions that update the master data? Master data forms an enduring record. The business needs master data to fulfil many purposes over time, and you never know when you are going to need it. On the other hand, we use the term 'transaction data' to mean the data about the activities that occur during a transaction. Every transaction generates a set of transaction data about itself.

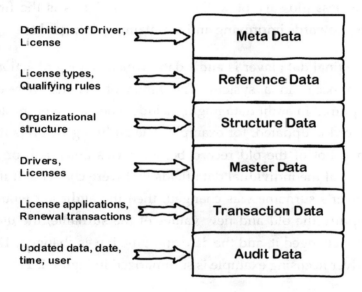

| | |
|---|---|
| Definitions of Driver, License | Meta Data |
| License types, Qualifying rules | Reference Data |
| Organizational structure | Structure Data |
| Drivers, Licenses | Master Data |
| License applications, Renewal transactions | Transaction Data |
| Updated data, date, time, user | Audit Data |

Figure 2-11 Six kinds of data involved in driver licensing

## Launching the payload

A metaphor may serve to illustrate the difference between master data and transaction data. The satellites and deep space probes that humans have launched in the last six decades or so are the pinnacle of technological achievement. Our ability to obtain high-resolution photographs of Pluto, or to steer a probe safely through the rings of Saturn despite a delay of 84 minutes in signal transmission between the craft to Earth, are astonishing achievements. The spacecraft that perform these extraordinary feats are freed from Earth's gravity and set on their path by huge and complex rockets.

Having set the craft on its journey, the rocket has done its job, and – apart from admiring the film footage of the launch – people quickly forget about the rocket and focus their attention on the spacecraft itself – the rocket's so-called 'payload'. The rocket has no purpose other than to set the payload on its proper course into space. However, sitting on the launchpad as the countdown progresses, the tiny payload is literally just the tip of the huge rocket iceberg.

During the launch process, a carefully timed sequence of operations is performed. Meanwhile, onboard sensors monitor every aspect of the machine in case any problems occur. Large amounts of data are generated by these sensors and computers examine the data, watching for unexpected anomalies that might indicate a problem that could jeopardize the mission. The launch team can suspend the pre-launch sequence if serious problems are detected; critical components can be replaced, or other adjustments performed; and the countdown then resumed when it is safe.

The whole process of launching a spacecraft involves hundreds of technical specialists and supporting staff. None of this myriad activity affects the precious payload, other than to keep it safe. The launch team's job is to successfully complete the 'transaction' of freeing the payload from Earth-bound gravity. Once their job is done, the launch team can relax. The transaction of launching the payload is finished.

Many components of the rocket's machinery and supporting equipment work together with many specialist launch teams. The craft to be launched into space is the sole reason for the entire exercise – the payload is like a business's master data. A business transaction is like the rocket, requiring a complex sequence of work, timing, and good error detection, but the only thing that is really carried on into the future is the 'payload' of master data. Without the payload, the transaction is pointless, like a rocket with no spacecraft in the nose cone. The rocket itself is like transaction data, storing data about the activities that occur during a business transaction.

## Managing transaction data better

Transaction data is comprised of the information that a business needs to capture, temporarily at least, about the activities that occur to move a business transaction along and to keep track of the transaction's status. The business operations teams use this data to manage the transaction through the various tasks they need to do to fulfil what the customer wanted.

For example, an order that needs to be fulfilled is a transaction. Historically, the order might come to the business on a handwritten or typed order form. The business might stamp it with the date received, add it to the stack of new orders, tick off the ordered items as they are picked from the stacks, and again as they are packed for shipment. In other words, in these manual systems, transaction data is recorded right on the paper order. The workers processing the order would have manual systems and procedures to ensure they did not misplace an order form, or neglect to pass the completed order form onto the billing team.

As we know, computer systems have changed the old ways of doing things. Nowadays, the customer might submit the order online, comprising a set of data about the order and the desired items. The business has processes – which may or may not be automated – to receive the order and relate it to a customer record, then to transfer the data to the warehouse for picking, packing, and shipping. The shipped order might be then passed over to the billing team for creation of an invoice which is sent to the customer.

The order record is transaction data. The order data contains information about who or what triggered the transaction, what the customer wanted, the status of the transaction, and so on. Typically, the business will use the order record itself to track the tasks that need to be undertaken, changing the status of the record as it progresses through the business process.

Some data about a transaction is specific to the type of transaction involved. An order for books will look quite different to an application for a driver's license. However, there is other transaction data that looks remarkably similar in structure no matter what type of transaction is being processed. Such generic transaction data holds information about the time and date on which the transaction was started and finished, the type of transaction it is, the tasks that have been performed on it, and the tasks that are yet to be started.

Some transaction data is not generic but is specific to the type of transaction being performed. In the case of an order transaction, the transaction-specific data includes the order form and the packing slip.

Now Emily realizes that data is important, and systems exist primarily to store and process data. Thinking about data needs should come before considering how best to sequence the business process. She understands that master data is data about important things like customers and products, and that master data has strategic importance to a business. Data about transactions is important in the short term, but eventually the business can forget about it – transaction data is important operationally, but not strategically. But Emily thinks that it is in the design of transaction processing where the efficiency and productivity of the business operation are determined. How can the design of transactions be simplified?

In Chapter 3 we will look deeper into transactions and their generic structure, while later in Chapter 6 we describe the generic data structures used to record the work activities involved in processing transactions.

---

## Three key points from this chapter

- Data lies at the heart of every business.

- Structuring your data well is the critical first step towards better systems and processes.

- The six kinds of data should be separated in your databases.

# Further reading

Carey, Craig. (2015) *The Origin of Writing*. Retrieved from: https://bit.ly/2Pdxetn (includes photos of tokens, bulla, tablets and cuneiform).

Davies, Lyn. (2006) "A is for Ox – A short history of the alphabet". Folio Society.

Hoberman, Burbank, and Bradley. (2009) "Data Modeling for the Business – A handbook for aligning the business with IT using high-level data models". Technics Publications.

# Responding to Requests

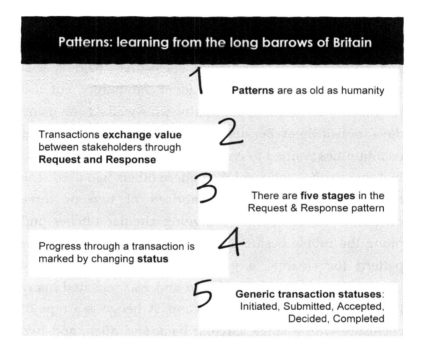

**Patterns: learning from the long barrows of Britain**

1. **Patterns** are as old as humanity

2. Transactions **exchange value** between stakeholders through **Request and Response**

3. There are **five stages** in the Request & Response pattern

4. Progress through a transaction is marked by changing **status**

5. **Generic transaction statuses**: Initiated, Submitted, Accepted, Decided, Completed

## People, patterns, and prehistory

People appreciate the value of a good pattern. With a desire to make something and a pattern in our hands, we are no longer starting with a blank sheet of paper. Instead, we have a tried and tested way to move forward. People have used patterns for centuries to achieve all kinds of purposes – sewing clothes, making metal tools, making furniture, building houses, getting married, developing software. Patterns are as old as humanity.

Consider for instance the people who inhabited Britain around 5000 years ago. They performed great earthworks that created new spaces in the landscape for socializing and ceremonies. These 'social enclosures' held special significance, not only for the resident community, but also for others outside the community who walked for many days to visit them. Because of this special meaning, other communities wanted to create their own social spaces and in doing so, they followed the pattern others had used. The earliest earthworks were comprised of two or three concentric circles made by digging circular ditches and piling the rubble beside them in a low bank. This simple pattern for creating a gathering place spread rapidly through the scattered population and was repeated many times in various parts of the island. A henge is a type of enclosure with a single circular bank and ditch, and two entrances opposite each other, as shown in Figure 3-1.

Later, a new pattern emerged in the same region for creating sacred burial places. Constructing a long barrow involved a more complex pattern requiring a multi-stage process – selecting a conspicuous site; finding, moving, and erecting stone slabs to construct a chamber of stone and a passage into it; then finally excavating from nearby a vast quantity of soil or chalk and piling it on top of the chamber.

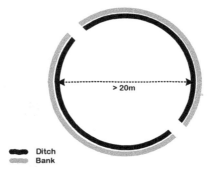

Figure 3-1 Pattern for a henge, c. 3000 BC

The pile of rubble was narrow and elongated – hence, 'long' – with ditches on each side that supplied the covering. The long barrow pattern was learnt and repeated many times over, from the south of England to Orkney and west to Ireland, but it was especially popular on the chalk downlands of the south, where the pile of white chalk created an unmissable gleaming landmark.

Figure 3-2 Standing stones guard the entrance to West Kennet Long Barrow, Wiltshire, England[6]

---

[6] Public Domain; https://bit.ly/2DHTCZL.

A third pattern that became popular was erecting circles of tall narrow stones. Like the circular banks and ditches, stone circles created special enclosed spaces for ritual gatherings and other communal activities, including midsummer and midwinter celebrations – the New Year's Eve of ancient times. Like the long barrow pattern, the stone circle pattern was deployed thousands of times far and wide throughout the British Isles.

Figure 3-3 Castlerigg Stone Circle, Cumbria, England[7]

The stone circle pattern and the circular bank and ditch henge pattern were sometimes combined, as shown in Figure 3-4, so that the structure could serve multiple purposes – e.g. as a social gathering place and an astronomical observatory. The henge-stone circle combination was employed on an immense scale at Avebury, shown in Figure 3-5.

---

[7] Ian Greig (https://bit.ly/2QdkasH), "Castlerigg Stone Circle - geograph.org.uk - 590652", https://bit.ly/1jxQJMa.

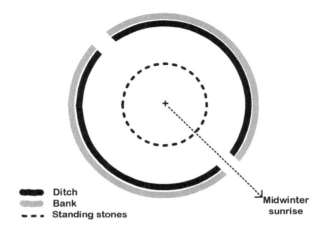

Ditch
Bank
Standing stones

Midwinter
sunrise

Figure 3-4 Pattern for a henge with stone circle

Figure 3-5 Avebury henge and stone circle, Wiltshire, England[8]

There were often local variants of the pattern that emerged as a result of the materials that were available, the character and position of the sites people chose for their enclosures, and community preferences. Long barrows became circular passage tombs in some places. Passage

---

[8] Blake Patterson from Alexandria, VA, USA (https://bit.ly/2RaGVuj), "Blakespot - henge at Avebury, County Wiltshire (by)", https://bit.ly/1ryPA8o.

tombs were built on a massive scale and included precise alignment to the solstice. Some stone circles included secondary circles made of different stones brought from further away. But in all cases, the established pattern is still recognizable – a stone circle or passage tomb in Orkney is remarkably like one located in Wiltshire or Cornwall.

Innovations also occurred now and again that changed the pattern significantly. Some of these innovations were one-off creative bursts, such as the famous and massive trilithons at Stonehenge, which were so resource-intensive and technically challenging that they were never attempted elsewhere. But those who followed the pattern closely could learn the techniques and borrow the necessary labor from other communities.

Like ancient Britons, modern businesses depend on established patterns for smooth internal operations and organization. In addition, businesses rely on other businesses to use similar patterns so they can conduct commerce with each other without needing to learn the ropes every time. Occasionally, a business invents a completely new way of operating and earning revenue – today we are very familiar with this through the many businesses which are leveraging digital technology to disrupt their industry and rapidly gain the lion's share of the market: Uber, Google, Amazon, Apple are examples. In some cases, these innovators are defining new patterns that others will follow, while others are building complex and enormous 'stonehenges' that may never be replicated.

In this chapter, we look at a simple pattern that is easy to replicate and can be applied to any business that transacts with customers – we call it the **Transaction Pattern**. But first, let's sit with Emily in one of her weekly meetings.

---

### Transaction Pattern

A generic pattern of processing phases and work tasks that can be applied to, and used to streamline, most types of business transactions.

---

Emily is annoyed. The weekly operational status meetings in her insurance claims department are so frustrating. The team leaders struggle to compile their reports and discuss their workloads and issues. One person turned up late because it took her an hour to assemble a report of her team's current work. Another team leader is complaining about going through this torture every week. During the meeting, it is almost impossible to work out whether a team has a lot to work on, or not. Why is this so hard?

Emily has noticed how agitated the department manager becomes when the three team leaders report on their workloads and seem to be talking in different languages. One person says, "We have 50 transactions in a finished state, and 23 in progress, 4 of which are blocked." Another team lead reports that "We have 37 new registrations come in this week and we have requested clarification from a third party on 3 of them. The other 34 have been done. Three new claims were reported this morning that we have not started." Emily wonders: Does 'finished' mean the same as 'done'? Does 'blocked' mean the same thing as 'requested clarification' or something else? Of the 23 newly received transactions, how many have not commenced processing yet? Is a 'registration' the same as a 'claim'?

Emily wonders why they don't use the same words to describe the work. If they did that, then it would be easier to compile an aggregated report showing the department's work in totality in one table or graph.

Are the processes for dealing with motor vehicle claims, house claims, and travel claims really so different? She knows that each process uses **status codes** to indicate where a transaction is up to in the process. The motor vehicle claim process has a status called 'Received' to indicate that information about an incident has been submitted by a claimant. A claim for a home and contents loss has a status called 'Lodged' to indicate that the application has been received but not yet processed. The process for lodgment of a travel claim uses a status called 'New' for the equivalent step.

> **Status codes** are simple words or abbreviations, such as 'Submitted' or 'SUB', used to indicate where a transaction is up to in a business process; they are a type of reference data.

This confusing situation is repeated with other status codes across the three processes, finishing the processes with 'Finished', 'Registered', and 'Done' depending on the type of insurance claim. In all, there are thirty different status codes across all three claim types.

Emily wonders whether the status codes could be made uniform across the three processes. This would reduce the number of status codes from 30 to 10, and Emily suspects those 10 could be simplified even further. For example, the statuses 'Approved' and 'Rejected' indicate the outcome as well as a stage in the process. To produce the weekly status report, the number of approved and rejected transactions need to be added together to give her the number of transactions that have been completed. Wouldn't it be simpler to have a single processing status of 'Decided'? The content of the decision (approval or rejection of the request) could be recorded in a separate field designed for that purpose, rather than embedded in the status code itself.

A smaller number of status codes, limited to standardized processing statuses, would certainly simplify the reporting and reduce the manager's confusion. This would also mean that the status reports from each team could be aggregated easily by adding up the numbers of transactions at each status. The manager could see the total workload and how it is divided between the teams. Emily thinks that if this happens, the status discussion would be so much more straightforward. The information could be displayed in real time as transactions occur, using a simple dashboard.

Emily thinks there must be a way to standardize the status codes in this way across the processes for all types of insurance claims. After all, the processes are not dissimilar. Perhaps the problem has arisen because the systems that support each process were built at different times by different developers. It is possible the developers made their own decisions about many aspects of the system design without considering the context of all the department's responsibilities and their need to be operationally efficient across all business lines.

## Business processes and the transaction pattern

Emily's insurance company processes a claim for vehicle damage differently than a claim for home contents theft, and differently again for travel claims. Emily cannot think why these claims have very different processes and why each business process is specific to a product.

Businesses often create distinct processes for each of their products. Often, this is the result of company mergers and acquisitions. But it is more likely that the processes have just evolved differently because separate departments manage the operations for each product. There is a significant cost to two (or more) different processes that do similar work. These unnecessary costs come from several direct costs, as well as lost opportunities such as: limiting staff mobility between departments and extra training costs, maintaining two computer systems, and creating data that is not easily compared between the product lines.

Businesses can save these unwanted costs by moving away from product-based processes towards a more generic process structure. A generic process can be applied to any of the company's products with minimal customization. The Transaction Pattern detailed in this book is one such generic process structure.

Using the Transaction Pattern, Emily will be able to strip away the product-specific variations from the processes so that the fundamental tasks that are performed on all product types are revealed. A generalized process like this is adaptable to new products and other changes in the business operations.

## Transactions comprise a request and a response

Every business service is an exchange between two stakeholders. There are two types of services:

A simple one-way provision of information – an **information service**.

A reciprocal exchange in which a mutually beneficial transaction occurs – a **transactional service**.

This book, for the most part, addresses transactional services, rather than information services. This is because most challenges facing computer system designers and business process designers lie in the complexity inherent in many transactional services, compared to the relatively straightforward provision of information. Also, patterns for information services are well-established in the website and web content design spheres.

As we described in Chapter 2, a transaction results in a change to the records of a business, whereas an information service does not. Our use of the term 'transaction' is broad and may or may not involve a financial transaction. 'Transaction' is a convenient label for any kind of exchange between stakeholders, including money, goods, licenses, and claims. Transactions also include updates to stored information, such as when a customer changes their address.

Typically, one stakeholder requests something of the other stakeholder, who decides what to do about the request and responds accordingly. Sometimes a transaction involves a customer requesting something from a business – for example, "I want to buy this book." Other times it is the business initiating a service with the customer – for example, "Here is our invoice; payment is due in 7 days."

Our use of the word 'stakeholder' here is deliberate. 'Stakeholder' is a neutral term that signifies that the customer, the business, or a third party may be the one making the request, or conversely responding to the request. In other words, sometimes the requester is a customer, but in other transactions the requester is the business. Which is which depends on the nature of the transaction.

Many transactions begin with a request from a customer, such as a product order or an application for a permit. We refer to these types of transactions as 'externally triggered'. Transactions that commence internally to the business include billing processes in which an invoice is generated and sent to a customer – essentially, an invoice is a request from a business who is owed money, with the expectation that the customer will respond with a payment. We call transactions that are commenced by the business itself 'internally triggered'.

Both externally-triggered and internally-triggered transactions are important and commonly occur in most businesses. For clarity in this chapter we will focus at first on externally-triggered transactions. The pattern for business-initiated, internally-triggered transactions is slightly different and is discussed separately later in the chapter.

Thinking more generally about different externally-triggered transactions, we can see that all types of transactions involve two distinct parts – first, a request from a customer, followed by a response from the business. Table 3-1 shows some examples to demonstrate this pattern of request-and-response.

Table 3-1 Examples of transaction requests and responses

| Customer Request | Business Response |
| --- | --- |
| Place an order for products with an online retailer | Assess the customer's eligibility to purchase; take the payment; fulfil the order; notify the customer that the order has been processed |
| Apply for a driver's license | Assess the applicant's eligibility and suitability to be a driver; fulfil the application; notify the licensee |
| Make a claim for an insured loss | Assess the claimant's eligibility; confirm/deny that the loss is covered by the policy; assess the loss; pay a settlement amount; notify the claimant |
| Apply for a loan to buy a house | Assess the credit worthiness of the applicant; issue a letter of offer to the customer |
| Order stock for a retail shop from a wholesaler on account | Pick, check, and ship the order; debit the retailer's account |
| Transfer funds from one bank account to another person's bank account | Check that the customer has sufficient funds to cover the transfer; issue a credit posting through the payment clearing house |

The feature common to all these examples is a clear break between the customer request and the business response. The requester has stated what they want. The second half of the transaction creates the business's response to that request.

## Transactions exchange value

The customer's request is offering up something that is of value to them in anticipation of receiving something else of value from the business in return. There is always such an exchange of value between the stakeholders. The end of a transaction is marked by the delivery of something of value to the customer – that is, the value they were seeking by interacting with the business. For example, a permit to do some regulated activity, the settlement of owed money, a product they wanted to buy, or confirmation that their recent change of name is updated.

In Table 3-2, we have suggested the value exchanged between the parties in the example transactions.

Knowing the value that is exchanged is very useful, as it enables us to identify individual services and to distinguish them clearly from other services within an end-to-end customer journey that may stretch across time and involve several distinct services. The delivery of the requested value marks the completion of a transaction.

Table 3-2 Examples of the value exchanged during transactions

| Customer Request | Business Response | Value Exchanged |
|---|---|---|
| Place an order for products with an online retailer | Assess the customer's eligibility to purchase; take the payment; fulfil the order; notify the customer that the order has been processed | Money ⇄ Goods and a confirmation |
| Apply for a driver's license | Assess the applicant's eligibility and suitability to be a driver; fulfil the application; notify the licensee | Personal information and a fee ⇄ A license to drive |
| Make a claim for an insured loss | Assess the claimant's eligibility; confirm/deny that the loss is covered by the policy; assess the loss; pay a settlement amount; notify the claimant | Information about the loss, including evidence ⇄ Money |
| Apply for a loan to buy a house | Assess the credit worthiness of the applicant; issue a letter of offer to the customer | Paying a higher rate of interest than the rate at which the bank borrowed the funds ⇄ The ability to buy a house |
| Order stock for a retail shop from a wholesaler on account | Pick, check and ship the order; debit the retailer's account | Promise to pay ⇄ Stock for the shop |
| Transfer funds from one bank account to another person's bank account | Check that the customer has sufficient funds to cover the transfer; issue a credit posting through the payment clearing house | The safe-keeping of funds ⇄ Convenience of making payments |

In a customer journey, this point is often a touchpoint between the business and customer, notifying them of the business's decision in response to the customer's request. Decisions are a vital element of a transaction.

> A **customer journey** or **service journey** is a comprehensive view, from a typical customer's perspective, of the events in their life that trigger interactions and transactions with a business.
>
> A **touchpoint** is when a customer and the business exchange information or conduct a transaction.

See Chapter 4 for more information about customer journeys and touchpoints.

## Transacting requires a decision

As well as passing between the request and the response stage, a transaction always involves a decision about whether the business can fulfil the customer's request, or not. In other words, will the business participate in this exchange of value with the customer? For example, an online retailer might confirm that it holds stock of the desired goods before it commits to accepting the customer's order. The bank makes a detailed assessment of an application for a loan and decides whether to offer a loan and on what terms. An insurance company will decide the monetary value of a customer's loss, based on the business rules that the company applies to the policy that the customer purchased. (Incidentally, the purchase of the policy is a separate transaction that must have occurred previously.)

The decision made by the business allows the transaction to reach closure, albeit not always to the customer's satisfaction. For example, a decision to not grant a driver's license (because the new driver failed a test) nevertheless completes the "Apply for a driver's license" transaction. We have added the decision that the business must make for each of the example transactions in Table 3-3.

The approval or decision action is often the clearest signal that a transaction is happening rather than an information service or a customer interaction. A customer journey may comprise many such decision actions. Identifying these decision points enables us to rapidly identify each distinct transaction within the end-to-end customer journey.

## Transactions follow a consistent pattern of changing statuses

These examples show that a consistent pattern, comprising a request from one stakeholder followed by a response from another stakeholder, commonly occurs in business transactions. Now let's look deeper into what lies within each of the request and response stages.

Table 3-3 Examples of decisions made during transactions

| Customer Request | Business Response | Decision | Value Exchanged |
|---|---|---|---|
| Place an order for products with an online retailer | Assess the customer's eligibility of purchase; take the payment; fulfil the order; notify the customer that the order has been processed | Can we fulfil this order? Has the customer paid? | Money ⇄ Goods and a confirmation |
| Apply for a driver's license | Assess the applicant's eligibility and suitability to be a driver; fulfil the application; notify the licensee | Is the applicant eligible and suitable? | Personal information and a fee ⇄ A license to drive |
| Make a claim for an insured loss | Assess the claimant's eligibility; confirm/deny that the loss is covered by the policy; assess the loss; pay a settlement amount; notify the claimant | What is a fair settlement amount for the reported loss? | Information about the loss, including evidence ⇄ Money |
| Apply for a loan to buy a house | Assess the credit worthiness of the applicant; issue a letter of offer to the customer | Is the credit risk acceptable? | Money lent at a higher rate of interest than the rate at which the bank borrowed it ⇄ The ability to buy a house |
| Order stock for a retail shop from a wholesaler on account | Pick, check and ship the order; debit the retailer's account | Can we fulfil the order? Is there a risk of bad debt? | Promise to pay ⇄ Stock for the shop |

All types of transactions are processed via a similar sequence of work activities. Each activity causes the status of the transaction to change. The status of a transaction is usually expressed in a single unambiguous word, or an abbreviation such as a three-letter code; for example, Submitted or SUB. Because it cannot exist in two statuses at once, the transaction clicks through a sequence of statuses one at a time, in response to the work that is performed on them.

We generalize these activities and transaction statuses to create a generic pattern that is applicable to many diverse transaction types. The example that follows illustrates how the generic pattern can be discovered amongst the details of a specific transaction. In the narrative below, the transaction's shifting statuses are shown in bold as we describe each phase of the transaction.

A typical example is an insurance claim, in which a policy holder notifies the insurer of a loss. You will notice that, in this illustration, the insurance claim transaction is described, at various points, as Initiated, Submitted, Accepted, Decided, and Completed. These are called transaction statuses. Every transaction moves through a defined sequence of statuses. The transaction's status tells the business what needs to be done next with the transaction. Thus, in the broader context of business operations, information about the current status of all active transactions is critical to managing the company's work.

During the **Request** half of the transaction, the customer initiates the transaction by identifying themselves to the insurer's website and selecting the type of loss they have experienced. The website may apply a profile of the customer, depending on what the insurer knows about them – e.g. a high-risk customer may be asked more questions about the loss than a low-risk customer. At this point a transaction has been initiated and we say that the transaction's status is now **Initiated**.

The customer then enters data in answer to a series of questions and attaches evidence in support of their claim (e.g. a death certificate for life insurance, photos of the damage in the case of property or vehicle insurance). The customer confirms these details and then submits the claim. The transaction has now reached a **Submitted** status.

Submitting the claim is, in effect, a request to the insurer to assess the claim and make a payment in recompense for the loss. Submission of the claim marks the end of what the customer needs to do, and it completes the **Request** half of the transaction.

Now it is the insurer's turn to respond. Until the transaction has been submitted by the customer, the website has not done very much other than retrieving and presenting information to the customer. However, once it becomes **Submitted**, the claim is transmitted to the back-office systems to be assessed. The insurer's back-office staff (or possibly an automated system) will validate the details and attachments provided by the claimant and match the claim to the relevant policy. If these validations pass, then the claim can now be accepted for assessment. The transaction's status moves from **Submitted** to **Accepted**.

The claim is then passed to an assessor, who assesses the loss, decides whether the claimant's policy covers the loss, and calculates its value. The status of the transaction now moves to **Decided**. The insurer will then notify the claimant of the assessor's decision and may execute a payment to settle the claim. The insurer has nothing more to do, as they have completed the response half of the transaction. The transaction status now changes to the final status in the sequence, **Completed**. In the above example, an Initiated insurance claim is in the customer's hands, until it becomes Submitted and the insurer receives it. A Submitted claim needs to become Accepted before the assessors can examine the loss and decide on the settlement amount. Once the claimant has been notified of the decision and the payment executed, the claim has been Completed. This sequence is shown in Table 3-4.

This example follows the same pattern no matter what type of insurance policy and type of loss are involved. In fact, the pattern is so common that most insurers employ a very similar pattern when they make attempts to standardize claims processing across their business.

Table 3-4 Changing statuses during a transaction

| Sequence | Activities | Generic Phase Name | Status during the Phase | Status at the end of Phase |
|---|---|---|---|---|
| 1 | Login, select claim type, apply customer risk profile | Initiate | Not applicable | Initiated |
| 2 | Enter data about the loss and attach supporting evidence | Submit | Initiated | Submitted |
| 3 | Validate that claim is complete and can be processed | Validate | Submitted | Accepted |
| 4 | Classify the claim, assign to assessor, assess value of loss, and approve or reject settlement | Decide | Accepted | Decided |
| 5 | Calculate payment, make payment, notify the claimant of the decision | Complete | Decided | Completed |

## A generic pattern of request and response

By detailing the process in the example above, we have identified that the transaction moves through a sequence of named statuses, as work is performed on it. By removing the specific details of the insurance claim transaction, we are left with a generic request-and-response pattern. The pattern comprises a progression of five transaction statuses interspersed between generic processing phases.

We have arrived at the basic request-and-response pattern that many transactions conform to. We call this generic pattern the **Transaction Pattern**. The Transaction Pattern is illustrated in Figure 3-6.

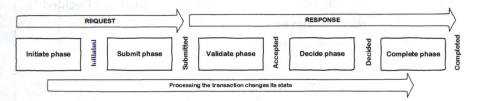

Figure 3-6 The generic Transaction Pattern for processing a transaction

Now, returning to Emily and her issue with the weekly operational status meetings. If all the transactions across Emily's department were to adopt the standardized statuses of the Transaction Pattern, the frustrations would disappear. Each team leader's reporting would be easy to interpret, because all reports are based on a common language, so to speak – everyone knows what Accepted and Completed mean. Measuring the volumes of active transactions in each of the five statuses would be a simple counting exercise, performed in minutes. We build up the details of the Transaction Pattern, and the benefits of using this pattern, in later chapters.

---

## Requests are resilient to changing response processes

The customer's request is very stable relative to the processes and systems that create the business's response. For example, a utility company will always receive certain requests from their customers, because people move to a new house, people cannot pay their bill, people want to know how much energy or water they have used, and so on. The information that the utility requires to process such requests remains remarkably constant over time. This means that the request needs to be resilient to any changes in back-office systems and processes.

For a century or so, people lodged their requests with the utility using the telephone or a paper form without much changing. Meanwhile, the utility's processing and recordkeeping methods may have evolved significantly over the same period. The pace of change has picked up with computerization and the digitization of services, but businesses need to be mindful that the request component of their transactions should be resilient to the frequent upgrades and replacements that they make to the computer systems. A business should be able to change something in the response part of a transaction without needing to also change the request part.

## Varying the transaction pattern

We have described so far in this chapter how a transaction comprises, at the highest level, a request from a stakeholder followed by a response from another stakeholder and looked into the details of the Transaction Pattern that applies to externally triggered transactions, in which a customer makes a request and the business responds. Now let's turn our attention to other scenarios, for example when the business initiates a request to a customer and the customer responds, and when a transaction is triggered by the arrival of a scheduled date. The Transaction Pattern readily adapts to these scenarios and – like any good pattern – can and should be varied to suit the nature of each transactional service. Firstly, we will look at making minor variations to the pattern to suit internally triggered transactions. The following section discusses three distinct pattern styles reflecting differing levels of complexity. These three styles can be used as the basis to find the right variation for a particular transactional service.

As we saw earlier in this chapter, an example of an internally-triggered transaction is customer billing, in which an invoice is generated and sent to a customer. Essentially, an invoice is a request from a business to a customer who owes the business money; the customer has an obligation to respond to the invoice with a payment. Billing and reconciling the payments received is a function that all businesses depend on for their financial viability and there are well-established and standardized approaches to performing the function, usually known as 'Accounts Receivable'.

Another group of internally-triggered transactions is scheduled transactions. These occur when an activity is scheduled to occur at a date in the future by being placed on a calendar of planned transactions. The scheduling of the future transaction is done at the end of an earlier transaction. When the scheduled date arrives, a new transaction is commenced by the business and a correspondence is sent to the customer informing them that there is an obligation that they must attend to.

The circumstances in which scheduling of future transactions might be necessary include the following:

- renewal of a permit or license
- review of an arrangement between the stakeholders, such as an individualized plan of in-home care

- activation of an extension clause in a service contract
- review of a customer's borrowings from a financial institution.

An internally-triggered scheduled transaction is typically commenced by sending the other stakeholder a notification to inform them that the business has commenced the transaction. You will have received notices telling you that your driver's license is due to expire, and you will need to renew it, by paying the fee and passing any required driving or knowledge tests. Similarly, people who receive financial or other support from government services are asked periodically to attend the office for a review of their support arrangement and their compliance with the obligations the arrangement places on them. These are internally-triggered transactions.

Sometimes, care is needed when discerning whether a transaction is internally or externally triggered. For example, an invitation from a government agency to apply for a round of grant funding may appear to be a transaction that is triggered internally by the agency. However, it is simpler to view the invitation to apply as an information service (called, say, *Invitation to apply for grant funding*), rather than the start of a transactional service. The customer is free to choose not to apply for a grant. So, if we regarded the invitation as the commencement of a transaction, the transaction would be left hanging forever if they did not apply. If they choose to apply, a transaction is initiated by the applicant – i.e. the transaction is externally triggered. There are two business services at work here, the invitation to apply (an information service) and the application itself (a transactional service).

The Transaction Pattern may need to be adjusted slightly for an internally-triggered transaction. One or two tasks may need to be moved from one phase to another, or some tasks removed altogether, however wholesale changes to the pattern should never be necessary. For example, in the case of a legal notice that should be approved by a senior solicitor before it is dispatched to the client, there may need to be a task added to the Submit phase to approve the notice. The task of identifying the customer could usually be omitted from an internally triggered transaction, as the identity of the customer is already known. In the case of a billing transaction, there is probably no need for a task in the Decide phase to approve the reconciliation of the amount received, since the relatively simple task of matching the amount of a payment with the amount due on the relevant invoice doesn't need a decision to be made, and the transaction can quickly move into the Complete phase.

## Three styles of transactional complexity

We have seen that transactions vary widely in their purpose, but all transactions involve a request and a response, passed between two stakeholders. The Transaction Pattern comprises a request from one stakeholder ("I want to open a bank account") and a response from another ("We have opened your new bank account. Your account number is ..."). The final thing to consider in this chapter is the varying complexity of processing required by differing transactions.

Emily knows that in her department the complexity of a transaction varies, from a simple information update that needs little or no processing to a complex sequence of tasks involving workflow and multiple interactions with the customer. Some transactions require very straightforward processing, while others require lengthy and complex business processes. Emily wonders if it is realistic to force-fit every transaction into a one-size-fits-all Transaction Pattern.

We saw in Chapter 2 how transactions update the business's master data. Some updates to master data need to be more controlled than others. In the case of a government agency, a transaction to update a customer's address may be straightforward and may not require any approval step. On the other hand, an update to the bank account of a welfare recipient may require verification and approval to mitigate the risk of fraud. Therefore the "update my address" transaction could be fully automated – or at least have minimal handling and certainly no approval step – whereas the "update my bank account" transaction would need to make its way or 'flow' through the pipelines of the work process to a verification officer (and possibly to a second approval officer).

The above examples suggests that there are three distinct types of transaction:

1. A direct style that can update the data records with no approval step.
2. A 'workflowed' style that involves a sequence of tasks that humans need to handle, possibly with the help of decision-making computer systems.
3. A case style that is more fluid.

**Direct style** – A direct update of data, not requiring Validate or Decide phases.

Figure 3-7 Direct style

The Direct style is suitable for updates to any master data that do not require checking or approval, such as updating addresses or other contact information.

**Workflowed style** – Tasks ordered in the common request-and-response pattern.

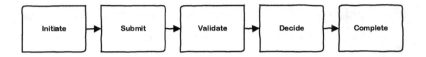

Figure 3-8 The intermediary 'workflowed' style

In the Workflowed style, a sequence of work tasks is followed, as we have described extensively in this chapter. This style allows for the possibility – indeed the probability – that different people may undertake each task. That is, tasks may pass from the workflow of one team into the workflow of another team.

The workflowed business tasks are sequenced in a repeatable, structured pattern. The tasks performed by both stakeholders follow a natural sequence that is similar across many transactions. Each task is assigned to a business role or team, either internally or externally. This allows not only for the customer to perform tasks, but also for external third parties to perform certain tasks, such as when an external payment service or credit check service is used within a transaction.

**Case style** – Some transactions are more complex than a simple linear sequence. This third style of transaction is more complex and dynamic. Tasks are selected, at the time of designing the workflow, in a sequence that is specific to the transaction. The tasks are still workflowed around the necessary teams, but not necessarily in a linear sequence like the Workflowed style.

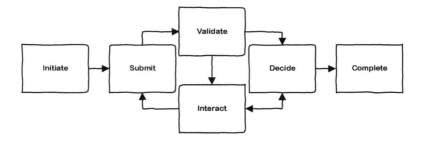

Figure 3-9 Case style

We call this more-complex transaction style the 'Case style', as it resembles the fluid nature of case management work. In case-like business processes, the process steps and tasks will vary between cases depending on their content and what happens while the case is active.

In complex transactions, the Case style allows the transaction designer to determine which tasks (selected from the master list of tasks) are required to process the transaction. The designer can then place the tasks in the necessary sequence. As in the Workflowed style, each task is assigned to a business role or team, either internal or external. During the operations of a Case style transaction, the tasks that the designer has selected are workflowed to the people and teams in the correct sequence.

An example of a Case style transaction is registration of a company, which requires a great deal of information to be exchanged with the registering authority. This can be a barrier to even starting the process for some applicants. To improve the customer experience, the registry might break the registration process into two stages. This might avoid the need for the applicant to provide all the required information upfront, as this would be unnecessary if the applicant were to fail to meet a qualifying criterion. The first stage would require only the qualifying information to be provided, while the second stage would seek more detailed information.

The service journey that stakeholders prefer may be as follows: initial qualifying check of basic information, followed by the submission and evaluation of further information, enabling a decision to be made. In this case, the designer would select a sequence of work phases such as the following:

1. Initiate
2. Submit A
3. Validate
4. Request for more information
5. Submit B
6. Evaluate
7. Decide
8. Complete

You will note that there are two Submit phases. These will be similar in form but will transmit different information. Both Submit phases involve the following: navigating to the correct place to enter information, responding to a set of questions, checking the responses, and submitting. The Validate phase will assess only the applicant's qualification for registration (by applying a set of business rules), while the Evaluate phase will assess the information that is sent in the second Submit phase.

This example is intended only to show that the selection and sequencing of the phases are flexible in the Case style of transaction. Another transactional service may need an entirely different sequence of work. For instance, applying to be enrolled in a government program for ongoing in-home support services, or seeking assistance with exporting goods to a new market, may require significantly different sequences of work phases.

We need to be cautious before using the Case style, however. It may be tempting to use the Case style because it can be made to closely align to an existing business process. This is a mistake, because this approach would mean that little streamlining of the business process would be achieved. On closer examination, we may find that the business process can be streamlined so that it fits the Workflowed style. This is a much better outcome for the business, as it simplifies the implementation and operational management of the improved process. It is worthwhile taking the time to work out whether the existing business process can be modified so that it conforms to the Direct or Workflowed style.

The Transaction Pattern provides a framework that constrains the types of work that can be performed in each of the five phases. A validation task can only occur in the Validate phase, while an approval task must occur in the

Decide phase. If two validation tasks are needed at different times in the work sequence, then the transaction needs to have two Validate phases. Mixing validation tasks in with other tasks that belong in a different phase will inevitably complicate the number of status codes that you need, and therefore lead to complex system implementations and, consequently, difficult operational management meetings. The work tasks within each phase may also be sequenced in a unique way that suits the needs of the transaction, yet this altered sequencing of tasks will not impact the transaction status that operates at the phase level rather than the task level.

The three transaction styles – Direct, Workflowed, and Case styles – give us a framework for taking transaction complexity into account and designing how a specific transaction should be processed in the most efficient manner.

Emily is thrilled to discover that her operational status meetings don't need to be as fraught as they have been lately. There is a way out of this mess! Every process needs to adopt a uniform set of statuses and adjust their process design so that there is a clear and unalterable sequence to the changing status codes. Processes can be released from being specific to one product and designed in a much more generic way, so that it doesn't matter which product is being handled. But how do we pay more attention to our customers' perspective? Can we have generic business processes while giving customers a good experience? How do we move work around the team efficiently and in a way that enforces adherence to the new set of status codes?

In the next chapter we look at the customer's perspective and how it is embedded in modern approaches to service design and customer experience.

---

## Three key points from this chapter

- People use patterns for many purposes because they help us do things faster and more consistently.

- The Transaction Pattern consists of five phases in its default Workflowed style: Initiate, Submit, Validate, Decide, and Complete. The status of a transaction changes at the end of each phase. The phases contain work tasks that may be automated or workflowed to human teams for execution.

- The Transaction Pattern is flexible and can be varied to suit the needs of a specific transaction.

# CHAPTER 4

# Experience the Service

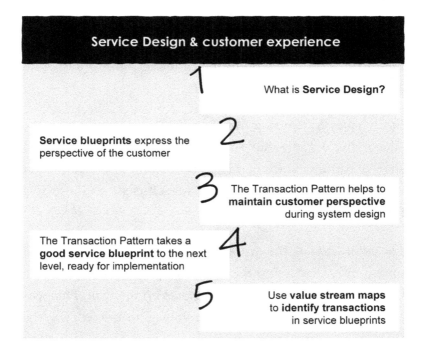

Emily has just attended a team training session on a new thing called 'Service Design'. Emily loves this new customer-focused approach and how it enables her to look at their business through the customers' eyes. Using journey maps showing the whole context of the customer's experience, she could better see why customers might think about using their services and what happens during and after the customers have transacted with the business.

Emily already knew that the various business functions in her organization act as if they are pretty much separate entities that perform their piece of a process. There was never much communication between these silos. No wonder customers fell through the cracks from time to time and experienced prolonged and frustrating interactions with several different teams while conducting a transaction.

Emily enjoyed learning how Service Design could help the silos in her organization to come together by focusing on a shared understanding of the customer journey and redesigning the journey to be more efficient and effective for the customer.

The attendees at the workshop spent a large part of the time jointly discussing the customer journey and building up the journey map with sticky notes on the wall. This was a useful way to get everyone involved in developing the customer journey collaboratively. Then they went further and added the interactions and transactions that occur at each touchpoint of the customer journey, building up detail as they explored the journey more. There were a lot of stickies on the wall by the end of the session.

All these efforts resulted in what the facilitator called a 'service blueprint' that provided a central reference for all the teams to apply in their improvement efforts. The blueprint seemed to Emily to be a simple and understandable map of a customer journey. She thought the service blueprint could be helpful in keeping people focused on the viewpoint of the customer, rather than their own internal viewpoint. For the customer journey that the workshop addressed, the service blueprint contained several touchpoints between customers and the business. Sometimes a touchpoint was a simple interaction or exchange of information, but at other points, the customer transacted with the business – that is, they were exchanging value.

Service Design seems like it could help the team to design better services and ensure that customers have a better experience. But Emily is confused about how Service Design could bring about a better design of each individual transaction – that is, a blueprint that can be used directly to communicate system requirements and process workflows. She thinks that the service blueprint doesn't go deep enough into the details. Although it is clearly a useful tool, Emily worries that her IT colleagues will find Service Design somewhat superficial; as such, it does not provide them with the requirements detail that they need.

While Service Design greatly helps to envision the desired customer experience and the way customers interact and transact with the business, it only goes so far. Service Design emphasizes the customer perspective more than the internal perspective. You still need to consider the internal processing needs and to specify the implementation details that will come together to make the service blueprint real.

Without this level of detail, the implementation project may lose something of the essence of the excellent Service Design work that has gone before it. The customer perspective is diminished, or perhaps the internal process journey is implemented in a clumsy manner that is little improvement on the old process. If either of these things occurs, then the supposed benefits of an improved customer experience, or of digitizing a service, will be lost.

The Transaction Pattern that we outlined in Chapter 3 corrects this imbalance and complements Service Design. **How does the Transaction Pattern tie in with a service blueprint, and how could Emily and her team use both methods alongside each other?**

## The Service Design approach

Your car mechanic offers services such as regular servicing. They may be good at their work and do an excellent job – this is the quality of their *work*. However, your mechanic may keep you waiting for weeks for an appointment, or fail to have the car ready when they promised, or be rude in their responses to your questions –

this is the quality of your *experience*. You are more likely to go back to a mechanic that minimizes the disappointments and emotional upsets of getting your car serviced, provided of course that the quality of their work is just as good.

So, the quality of the experience that the customer has is an important extra dimension of a service. Businesses that want to facilitate a pleasant, productive, or effective experience for their customers will pay considerable attention to the customer experience and what emotions are engendered, as much as the services themselves. To enable this focus on customer experience, practitioners have developed an approach called 'Service Design'.

Service Design is a new approach to designing business services emphasizing the customer's viewpoint. The approach recognizes that as well as designing the business's products (tangible things like cars and appliances, as well as financial products, contracts, and so on), the business should also design the service and the desired experience that accompany a product. Businesses that fail to recognize this, usually offer a terrible experience to their customers. For example, two shops may sell identical products, but the customer's experience of the shops' service may be vastly different. The differing experience of the retail services is a key factor in which shop the customer chooses to buy from.

The development of the Service Design approach is a response to important trends in the early 21$^{st}$ Century. These social, economic, and technological trends are creating pressures on businesses to operate differently than how they have in the past. Customers are expecting better service, including through convenient digital channels. As we explored in the Introduction, these trends demand that established businesses adopt new operating models. Not only does the customer experience need to be modified and streamlined, but the whole modus operandi of the business needs to change to align with the desired customer experience. A new operating model does not simply evolve but must be designed. Service Design offers a method for approaching the problem, by ensuring that a focus on the customer is front and center of the new model.

Service Design takes a 'big picture' view of the journeys that customers engage in. These journeys involve various touchpoints between the customer and the business, at which the customer obtains information from, or interacts and transacts with, the business or government service.

Service Design offers a variety of tools that can be used in combination to design a service. Developing customer profiles and interviewing to obtain customer insights are used to gain information about the experience that customers have within their context. This information is then used to create customer journey maps, which visualize the touchpoints that customers have with the business, through selected channels, at different phases from becoming aware of a service, to joining and using the service, through to leaving the service. Customer journey maps often include notes about how a typical customer might feel at each touchpoint. Customer journeys are an illustration of the experience that a customer has.

There is a wide and rich variety in the styles of customer journey map, from the simple and general, to the detailed and specific journey that a real person (in the form of a persona) undertakes. Figure 4-1 is a template for a less complex journey map, while a more complex example is shown in Figure 4-2. The key is to select a style that is appropriate for your context and what insights you want to gain from the map. Many creative designers have made graphically complex customer journey maps that seek to engage the viewer while conveying a lot of information. An internet search for "Customer journey map example" will return hundreds of examples; examining them may help you identify a good style to use in a particular instance.

Typically, a customer journey map depicts the journey horizontally as a sequence of stages. Each stage is subdivided into the steps or activities that the customer performs. Some activities will involve a touchpoint with the business, but many will not. These latter activities serve to remind the service designers of the customer's context including what other tasks they might perform while transacting with the business.

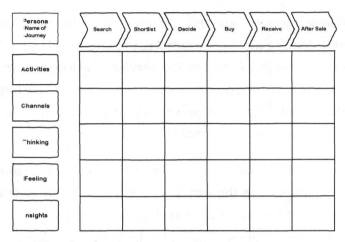

Figure 4-1 Template for a customer journey map

Various vertical layers are added to each stage of the journey, such as what the customer is thinking and feeling, the channels used for each touchpoint, and insights gained through user research about opportunities to improve the customer experience. The thinking and feeling layers attempt to portray the customer's thoughts at each stage and their emotional response – e.g. whether they are happy with the experience or frustrated by it. The emotional responses are often shown graphically to represent the ups and downs of the customer's feeling.

A customer journey map can then be used to delve into the detail at each touchpoint to redesign it for a better experience. In contrast to business process maps, which are internally oriented, a customer journey map shows what customers do and their interactions with the business, not what happens behind the façade of the touchpoints.

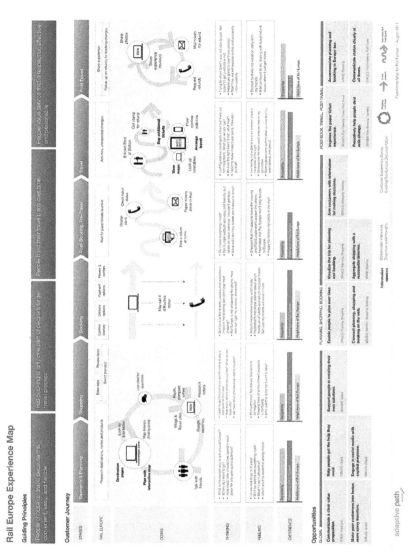

Figure 4-2 An example of a customer journey map[9]

[9] Rosenfeld Media from Brooklyn, USA (https://bit.ly/2r9ftBX, „SD053-Figure 5.14 (8462249080)", https://bit.ly/1ryPA8o.

Customer profiles and insights can be generalized or fictionalized in the form of personas and service scenarios. Each service scenario features a clearly defined context, customers, staff, brands, and motivations. Scenarios are most useful for trying out different future state service designs, by testing them against a few 'real' scenarios. This is an effective way to assess whether a new design is an improvement for a range of customer types and contexts. The new service blueprint can be tweaked on the fly to suit each service scenario better. This is a very low-cost way to settle on an improved service design.

Another Service Design tool is called 'organizational impact analysis'. This is a tool for examining the effect of a customer-facing change on the internal operations of the business. It asks: What do we need to change internally to deliver this improved customer experience – which business processes, procedures, team structures, systems and databases? How significant are these changes? How much effort will the change require to realize the new experience? Understanding the extent and complexity of this impact of change is critical to implementing a change successfully. Service Design assesses change impact by drawing connections between the customer experience and the service delivery functions and capabilities. This helps with defining which functional units, business capabilities, processes, and policies will need to be updated. Furthermore, by aligning these change impacts to the customer journey, it is clear which touchpoints will be affected if an impact is only partially implemented, or not at all.

Finally, a key tool of the Service Design approach is design workshops. Workshops are highly collaborative and creative exercises, in which participants engage actively. Templates are used to structure the conversation and to capture the insights. Design workshops are used at multiple points throughout a change initiative, but the focus of each workshop will vary. It is important that design workshops are not simply a one-off event, but a series of events that bring people together regularly. This ensures that a common vision is shared, while enabling the design of the service to evolve as understanding is enhanced and complexities are exposed.

The focus of a workshop may be to understand a situation or a problem, to capture and share what is known about customers' current experience and problems with using a service that needs improvement. Also, this workshop style can be used to identify unmet needs and gaps in the current service offering that present an opportunity for innovation. Another workshop style is to imagine new concepts for improvements that could be made to services. Service scenarios are often developed in this style of workshop, bringing ideas to life. This enables new ideas to be evaluated against the customer scenarios that are likely to be encountered when the improved or new service is operational. The third style of workshop is to design a detailed view of a service blueprint based on a new concept.

These design workshops develop front office and back office views of the proposed service, working across channels and business functions. The result is a comprehensive map of the service that provides a shared understanding to all teams involved in building or operating the service. Workshops may also be used to govern the build of multiple project components to maintain alignment with a consistent customer experience and goals. No matter the focus of a workshop, all workshops bring together multidisciplinary teams who contribute their individual perspectives to a common shared vision.

A proposed service design is mapped in the form of a service blueprint that visualizes the customer journey alongside the channels and front office actions that customers will engage with at each touchpoint. Service blueprinting techniques have been studied and formalized to an extent, but they do not need to use complex notations; blueprints can be expressed using simple and easily understood graphics.

The service blueprint, like the customer journey map, is anchored on a horizontal sequence of customer activities. The customer's viewpoint of their journey drives everything else. Aligned with each of the customer activities there are actions taken by front office employees.

These actions may vary according to the channel that is used for the interaction (face-to-face, phone, email, or website). Beneath the front office actions are the supporting activities that occur in the back office that customers do not interact with directly. A line of visibility should be added to the blueprint to draw attention to what customers are aware of and what is invisible to them. Finally, the documents, websites, vouchers, and other artifacts that customers receive or provide at each touchpoint (often referred to as 'physical evidence') are noted on the blueprint. The diagram in Figure 4-3 shows an example service blueprint.

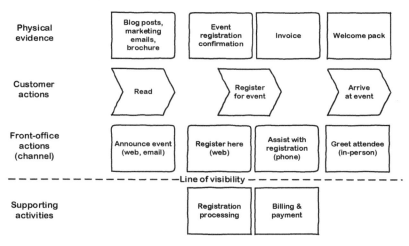

Figure 4-3 Example service blueprint for event registration

The service blueprint can be extended to include the organizational functions that perform work behind the scenes and in supporting roles. Also, the business capabilities that are required to deliver the service can be included in the blueprint. Furthermore, operational measures and other factors can be added to the blueprint. These might include timing of activities or the minimum timeframe that customers expect, any existing failure points, and points at which excessive waits occur.

Figure 4-4 is an example of a service blueprint that shows how the organizational functions are aligned with each of the steps in the customer journey.

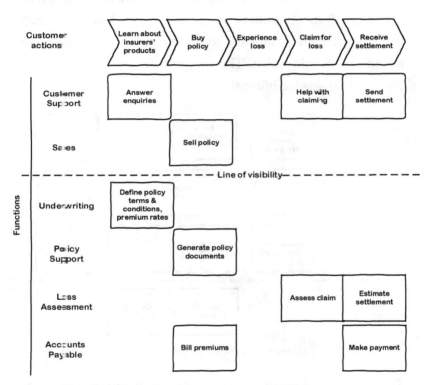

Figure 4-4 Service blueprint with organizational functions

Service Design takes a broad view of what a service is. Services comprise many information exchanges, transactions, and other interactions across a customer journey. The service blueprint shown in Figure 4-4 includes an information service (providing information about insurance policies) and two transactional services (buying the policy and making a claim). In addition, Customer Support facilitates several interactions that help to move along the information and transactional services.

Take a telephone company for instance. The products offered by a telecommunications company include fixed line telephone, mobile phone, and broadband internet products. When a customer explores, buys, and uses a fixed line telephone product, the company will give them information about the product, possibly at multiple points in the journey. The customer will interact with the business through various channels (e.g. retail shop, phone, and online) and they will transact with the business in several different ways. The transactions include the initial purchase and contract signing, paying monthly bills, setting up the product in the home, addressing faults and other technical issues, and eventually withdrawing from using the product.

Each time the customer transacts with the telephone company a separate transaction occurs. Each transaction, from its initiation by the customer to the response by the company, will follow the Transaction Pattern described in this book. Therefore, the Transaction Pattern applies at a more specific and detailed level than the service blueprint.

# A service blueprint sets the context for transaction design

Service Design's customer focus contributes a perspective that is often missing from projects tasked with redesigning business processes or developing enhancements to information systems. This aspect alone means that significant value can be gained from the Service Design approach. Using service blueprints enables the surrounding context of each transaction to be readily shared and understood by everyone involved in a project, even when the project's scope is limited to one transaction type among several in the customer journey.

A service blueprint highlights the point where the customer transacts. Certain touchpoints in the customer journey are the points at which transactions start or finish. Using these touchpoints as markers, the blueprint can be segmented into distinct transactions. Information exchanges and other interactions occur between the transacting touchpoints. An alternative style of a service blueprint that shows this clearly is a simple expression of a customer journey, aligned to three separate rows showing the information services, transactions, and other interactions that the customer engages in at each touchpoint of the journey. This is a straightforward way to understand and communicate two very important pieces of information: the point where the customer seeks information or interacts through a channel, and the point where the customer initiates or completes a transaction with the business. This style of service blueprint is illustrated in Figure 4-5.

This technique allows us to home in on one transaction that needs improvement, while being aware of the context in which it is used by the customer and the internal actions and capabilities that support the transaction. This is a useful perspective to keep at the forefront of the subsequent design and development work.

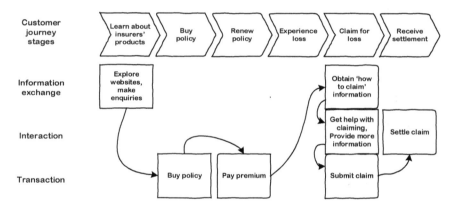

Figure 4-5 Customer journey showing the flow of information, interaction, and transaction touchpoints

The thorough understanding obtained from the service blueprint is an excellent foundation for subsequent detailed system and process design work. A service blueprint, however, is not enough to begin development of the systems needed to implement the blueprint. If it were used in that way, the business and functional requirements of the system would be elaborated through user stories using an Agile development approach. This is a common approach, but it has a significant disadvantage because it lacks architectural underpinnings. Although the user stories may be entirely consistent with the service blueprint, they are isolated features that are difficult to align to a coherent architecture of the full business solution. It is like building part of a house with some knowledge of how that room will be used, but no knowledge of the overall architecture of the house. Awareness of the full architecture ensures that the house has integrity and functions well as a whole. The risk of going into software development armed with a service blueprint and user stories alone is that the business solution solves an immediate problem but creates systems and data structures that lack integrity. This can lead to downstream problems. Subsequent remediation exercises to fix these issues are inevitable in time.

Since Service Design focuses largely on a customer-needs, outside-in perspective, the approach can only make a limited contribution to the detailed specification of how transactions are initiated and processed. By 'detailed specification', we are referring to the precise data requirements, business rules, and workflows that enable a transaction to be received and processed efficiently (with minimal cost and time) and effectively (the customer achieves their objective and the policy is complied with). On the other hand, Service Design and the Transaction Pattern are highly complementary. The products of the

Service Design approach can be used alongside the Transaction Pattern described in this book to deliver a coherent and comprehensive specification. Detailed transaction design builds on the foundation of the higher-level Service Design activities. Combining these two methods makes for a highly effective design process that results in a design that has a strong customer focus while also giving structure to the detail that is required for implementation.

Service Design points to how the customer experience of a service can be streamlined to fulfil the customer's objective more efficiently, through better exchanges of information, more effective interactions, and smoother transactions. This results in a service blueprint that provides a strong foundation for more detailed design work. Following on from the Service Design activities, the Transaction Pattern will support you in going to the next level of design. The Transaction Pattern provides a framework to specify the necessary data, business rules and workflow that govern the business operations for each type of transaction. Requirements definition workshops can be structured on templates derived from the Transaction Pattern and conducted in a similar way to the Service Design workshops. (In Chapter 9, we suggest how transaction requirements workshops can be managed in such a structured fashion.)

Developing this level of design detail is only necessary when the need for change, either in systems or processes, has been identified, perhaps through the Service Design work or through strategic investment planning. It may not be necessary to specify the detailed design of all transactions in a blueprint all at once. Indeed, trying to do too much at once raises the overall risk of project failure. Each transaction can be specified, built, and implemented independently. The result will be one or more transaction designs, each based on the request-and-response pattern, that can then be implemented into systems and business operations. Each transaction is employed at the appropriate touchpoint in the service blueprint that was agreed upon earlier during the Service Design work.

The complexity that is often inherent in sophisticated business systems and processes will become more manageable using this two-fold approach. The specification of each transaction will be laid out in a coherently structured end-to-end design yet separated from the specification of other transactions. The service blueprint holds the separate transactions together, by providing an easily understood customer-centric map showing the full context of each individual transaction.

## Identifying transactions

We have seen in this chapter how a customer's journey may comprise many transactions and information exchanges. To understand the customer journey fully, we need to partition it into these separate services, so that we know where one transaction starts and finishes. Such analysis of a customer journey can sometimes prove to be difficult, as a transaction may be spread over several touchpoints, or two transactions might be muddled together in one touchpoint. Two techniques may be helpful to clearly distinguish one transaction from another: Looking for activities that change master data, and mapping value streams. Let's investigate each of these tools.

## Tool #1: Follow the master data

A transaction will usually create or update only one type of master data. In the *Apply for license* example in Chapter 2, the master data being created is a *Driver license* record. On the other hand, if the service user does not provide any data to the business, then the service is almost certainly an information service – there is only a one-way exchange of information. Each touchpoint in a customer journey has a unique purpose, with information passing between the customer and the business. The key to marking the beginning and end of a transaction is to figure out whether any master data is altered at each touchpoint of the customer journey. Oftentimes, a touchpoint will be an interaction that is needed to move the transaction along, such as a request for more information, a progress notification, or a status update. Other touchpoints will clearly commence a new transaction or complete a transaction. These kinds of touchpoints are useful markers for dividing a journey into discrete services.

## Tool #2: Value stream mapping

The flow of information exchanges and transactions shown in Figure 4-5 corresponds to the services offered by the business. When these services are arranged in a linear series, we can see that each service delivers some value to the customer and adds to the value delivered by the previous services. This series of value-delivering services is called a 'value stream'. A value stream represents clearly and concisely what the organization is in business to do, what value it delivers to its customers – that is, the business's value proposition. Unlike a customer journey map and service blueprint, a value stream is usually expressed with an internal perspective, rather than a customer perspective. They are diagrammed as a simple map, such as the map shown Figure 4-6 for credit card services.

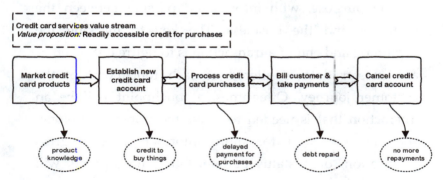

Figure 4-6 Value stream for credit card services

This example also indicates the value that customers derive from each service in the series and the overall value proposition.

While the content of the value stream map bears a close resemblance to the customer journey map, they are not the same. Figure 4-7 shows a customer journey map for obtaining and using a credit card.

Figure 4-7 Customer journey for getting and using a credit card

You will note that the active verbs used in the value stream in this example (Market, Establish, Process, Bill, and Cancel) show a perspective that is internal to the credit card provider. On the other hand, the verbs used in the steps of the customer journey (Learn, Apply, Receive, Use, Repay, and Close) portray the customer's perspective. That is, the two sets of verbs mirror each other. This is no accident and reflects the close relationship between the customer journey, in which the focus is on the customer's experience, and the more business-like value stream with its internal perspective.

The activities in the customer journey should align closely with the services in the value stream map. This alignment is illustrated in Figure 4-8. Using this alignment, we can then identify whether each service in the value stream map is a transaction or provides information only. In this case, we can identify an information service by which customers learn about the bank's credit card products, and three transactional services, as follows:

- Processing a new credit card application
- Billing each month for purchases and interest charges
- Cancelling a credit card account.

The Transaction Pattern is used to specify and implement each of the transactions.

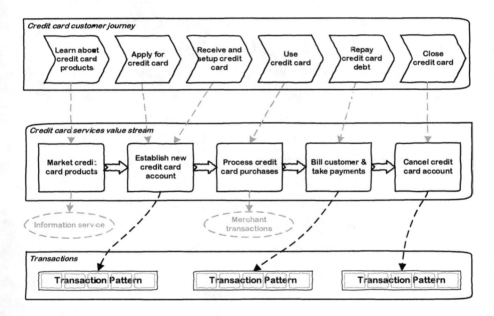

Figure 4-8 Customer journey aligns to value stream

In this way we can build up a complete picture of the customer journey, the transactions the customers use at various points, and the value that they receive. By analyzing the alignment of the customer journey with the value stream, we can not only improve the journey map itself, but also identify every transaction and information service that exists in the business. Using a diagram such as this during a process improvement initiative or system redevelopment project enables people to retain a strong awareness of the business context of a transaction or of a component of a transaction. The map allows the reader to rapidly orient themselves to the business context, so they are aware of where the current topic of discussion fits in the entire journey.

In Figure 4-8 we can see that the customer journey, the transactions and information services, and the Transaction Pattern unite to deliver the desired customer experience and value. This alignment means that the customer perspective is always present when it comes to specifying the business requirements for a transaction when using the Transaction Pattern. So far, such as in Figure 4-7 and Figure 4-8, we have seen how a value stream map illustrates a high-level picture of the value stream, which is useful for obtaining a rapid overview. However, to be useful as an input to projects more detail is required. We need to describe each service of the value stream in a less-ambiguous manner than a mere label such as 'Establish new credit card'. Also, we need to understand more precisely what each service produces and what stakeholders are involved.

Fortunately, there is a formalized, structured way to express a value stream in more detail, including: what triggers it, what occurs within it, and what is produced by each service of a value stream. Each service is given a name and description, entrance and exit criteria, the item of value that is produced, and the external and internal stakeholders who are involved.[10]

For example, the bank's value stream illustrated in Figure 4-6 is called *Credit Card Services* and the value proposition is: *Readily accessible credit for purchases* (i.e. the value that the customer would expect from using the services). As shown above, there are five services, or 'value stages', in this value stream. One of these services – *Establish new credit card account* – is defined formally as 'Receiving an application, validating, approving, issuing, and activating a new credit card'. The stakeholders involved are the customer and the bank's front office staff, Card Services, Card Production & Dispatch. The entrance criterion is that the application for a credit card is initiated, while the exit criterion is that the new credit card has been issued and activated by the bank. The value to the customer is that they know that they now have preapproved credit up to a certain limit to buy goods and services. In a similar fashion, the remaining stages of the *Credit Card Services* value stream are defined, as shown in Table 4-1. (The table

---

[10] See *BIZBOK Guide*, Business Architecture Guild,
   https://bit.ly/2FTS01M.

can be used as a template for this purpose when formally describing any value stream.)

The structure described above to fully define a value stream imposes a discipline that prevents some types of errors. For example, if you cannot define the value that the customer receives from a service in the value stream, then you have most likely identified only part of a service – you have broken down the value stream too much.

Take it up a level until you can clearly define the entrance and exit criteria and the value achieved for the customer. For example, a step that only validates the customer's address is unlikely to deliver any value to the customer (they already know their address), so the service must do more. The right level is reached when you can clearly see a request followed by a response that delivers the value sought by the customer.

In the next chapter we look at some concepts from business architecture and how these can help to bring greater elegance and integrity to your work on a specific transaction. In Chapter 9 we suggest a method for discovering and documenting requirements for a transaction. The method utilizes an interactive workshop style similar to Service Design techniques.

Table 4-1 Analysis of the Credit Card Services value stream

| | Value Stream: Credit Card Services | | | Value Proposition: Readily accessible credit for goods and services | |
|---|---|---|---|---|---|
| Service/ Value stage | Market credit card products | Establish new credit card account | Process credit card purchases | Bill customer & take payments | Cancel credit card account |
| Description | Prepare and publish consumer information about credit card products | Receiving an application, validating, approving, issuing, and activating a new credit card | Receiving, validating and settling merchant payments | Tallying the month's credit card activity, calculating interest and minimum repayment, sending a statement to customer, and receiving repayment | Initiating and processing a request to cancel a credit card account |
| Entrance criteria | Need for marketing identified | Application initiated | Purchase is made by customer at merchant | Billing cycle start date | Cancellation request initiated |
| Exit criteria | Marketing material received | Activated new account | Payment to merchant received | Monthly repayment received | Closure of credit card account |
| Value item | Knowledge of credit card products | Preapproved credit to buy things | Goods & services purchased on credit | Debt repaid | No more repayment obligations |
| Stakeholder | Customer, Marketing, Front office staff | Customer, Front office staff, Card Services, Card Production & Dispatch | Customer, Merchant, Card Settlements | Customer, Card Billing | Customer, Front office staff, Card Services |

## Three key points from this chapter

- Service Design has a lot to contribute to improving services, systems and processes, by emphasizing the customer perspective.

- A Value Stream provides a mirror to a service blueprint through documenting the internal perspective and objectives of a set of business services.

- The Transaction Pattern complements both Service Design and Value Stream Mapping, by taking a specific transaction to a deeper level of detail while retaining clear sight of both the customer perspective and the internal perspective.

## Further reading

Mager, Birgit. (2018) *Introduction to Service Design - What is Service Design?* Retrieved from: youtu.be/f5oP_RlU91g.

Reason, Ben; Løvlie, Lavrans and Flu, Melvin Brand. (2016) "Service Design for Business". Wiley.

*Service Blueprint* in Wikipedia. Retrieved from https://en.wikipedia.org/wiki/Service_blueprint.

*A key to service innovation: Services blueprinting;* W.P. Carey School of Business, Arizona State University. Retrieved from https://bit.ly/2BKSrr3.

CHAPTER 5

# Grand Designs

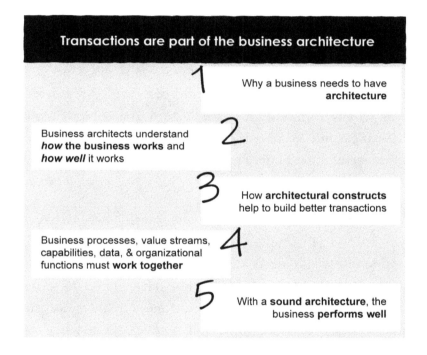

"The architects won't let us do that!", Emily heard someone mutter darkly. Emily wondered, who are these all-powerful architects? Are they the thought police? When she asked her colleagues about what the architects do, they answered vaguely. No one seemed to know what the architects did exactly, but everyone knew they could say 'no' to anything that was 'not part of the architecture'.

Emily wants to know more about these authoritarians. After all, she had worked with an architect on her new house recently and he was far from autocratic. In contrast, he stimulated her thinking, opening her mind to layouts and features that she had not considered previously. Her confidence in the architect grew as they discussed the design concepts for the house, the architect coming back with modifications and new ideas at each session. He gently explained to her why an idea she put forward might not work so well as a livable space, or perhaps needed stronger structures that would add cost to the project. He was willing to modify the architecture to accommodate a new idea, but he also highlighted the cost impacts and other factors that Emily needed to consider as the owner of the house.

When it came time to build the house, her architect worked with the builder to clarify elements of the design, and to resolve issues that the builder thought would be too difficult to build. Emily could not have hoped to work directly with the builder without her architect as the intermediary – she didn't have enough knowledge of building or even the right language. He seemed to know how to communicate effectively with both her – the client – and the builder. It struck Emily that the architect seemed to have an important role as the intermediary throughout the detailed design and building process.

If buildings need architects, then it made sense to Emily that complex businesses would need them too. Without architects, all the moving parts of a business could be put together badly, and not pull in the same direction, so to speak. Why did her colleagues seem to think that the architects were only there to block their ideas? What was 'the architecture' they spoke of, anyway? Had anyone ever seen it? How were Emily and her colleagues supposed to know that the architecture was what they – the clients in the client-architect-builder trio – actually needed? Would her colleagues stand for it if they were left out of the conversation about their new house, and instead the architect and builder built what they alone wanted, as if they were going to live in it? John Nutt, head of the engineers for the Sydney Opera House, pointed to the close relationships that make for a successful building project. The same idea also applies to business projects.

*On any building, the greatest collaboration comes from that sympathetic relationship which the architect, the engineer and the client feel for each other.* [11]

## Form and function

*The fundamental task of an architect is finding the form that will accommodate the purpose of the building. Complex functions are difficult to define at first, but tend to clarify*

---

[11] John Nutt, Chairman of Arup Australia, in *Building a Masterpiece – the Sydney Opera House*, ed. Anne Watson, Powerhouse Publishing, 2006.

*and diverge during design and, over extended time, evolve in*
*conflict with the framework they inhabit.*[12]

The beautiful white shells projecting into Sydney Harbor catch the eye and take the breath away. The alluring vision beckons us to go inside, look around, and perhaps attend a performance. As the Sydney Opera House vividly demonstrates, the form of a building invites engagement with it. As well as form, all buildings must also have function – they are built to fulfil a purpose. The function of the building may not be obvious from its form, but the form must be right for its intended function. Needs change over time and the function of the building must evolve, yet the building's form is more difficult to change.

Figure 5-1 Sydney Opera House[13]

---

[12] Ken Woolley, *Reviewing the Performance: the design of the Sydney Opera House*, Watermark Press, 2010

The Sydney Opera House dramatically demonstrates this truth. Once the structural form of the famous shells had been constructed, it became hugely problematic to change the function of the interior spaces – but that's exactly what happened. The building's client decided to change the function of the main hall from opera to concert performances after detailed design and construction had been underway for some years. The architect was faced with the extraordinarily difficult task of designing new interiors within the now-complete and unalterable structural form, with only limited success. These evolving functional requirements added a huge extra cost and delay to the project before it was even open. A completely new architecture was required for the interior spaces. Acoustic and other problems have plagued the building as a result. Further evolutions in function have emerged over the years since the Sydney Opera House was opened in 1973, making consequent – albeit less drastic – modifications to the building's form necessary.

The 'form' of a website also invites a browsing customer to engage with it; you feel drawn to a website that is engaging. On the other hand, you may feel turned away by a website that looks uninviting or makes it difficult to find what you want. Getting the 'form' of the website just right is the first job of user experience designers. But the

---

[13] Alex Proimos from Sydney, Australia (https://bit.ly/2zq1USX), "In the Sails of the Opera House (6619486933)", https://bit.ly/1ryPA8o.

experience that users feel when they interact with the website is merely a facade of the actual business, like the foyer of a building. The foyer of the Opera House fulfils a necessary function, but a function that is subsidiary to the 'main event' of the performance halls. The functions that go on inside the 'form' of a business are dominated by the operations in the business's back office, away from the eyes of the customer, who don't know or care about them – unless it results in a terrible service, of course.

A complex business supports many intersecting functions, just like a complex building. The performances that occur in the Sydney Opera House rely on many non-public spaces and systems: the dressing rooms, rehearsal spaces, stage apparatus, power supply, air conditioning, communications systems, and so on. The concert patrons care nothing of these matters – that is, unless something goes wrong that affects the quality of the performance. Maybe the lights go out midway through a performance. Maybe the performer in their dressing room was not communicated with and misses their cue.

The 'back office' systems that enable a theatre to host a performance without such hiccups, or worse disasters, will be familiar to any experienced performer, stage manager, producer, musical director, and lighting director, even when they have never used that theatre before. The systems are based on well-established patterns used in theatres throughout the world. These patterns enable a crew to 'bump-in' to an unfamiliar venue and put on a flawless show, albeit perhaps masking any creaks and groans from the eyes of the audience.

Likewise, the back stage of a business also relies on patterns that are familiar across many different businesses. For example, the accounting, ordering, billing, and payments processes and systems will be familiar to a new member of staff in the finance team. The back-office functions, and perhaps even the front office, will "evolve in conflict with the framework they inhabit", just as the functions of the Sydney Opera House evolved considerably from the initial brief to the architect.

Fortunately, it is easier to evolve a business's front office to meet these evolving needs when it is built in furnishings and software, rather than pre-stressed concrete. A website's 'form' can be readily changed or completely rebuilt to accommodate new functions. However, the back office has a structural form that is not so easy to change quickly. The 'structural form' of the back office is too-easily hard-wired into complex information systems by the system development practices commonly in use. For this reason, the funding required to modernize complex processing systems is often eye-wateringly large. So, when changes to the business's 'function' are required – say, a new business line, a new compliance requirement, or a streamlined business process – a significant and costly change to the 'form' of the information systems becomes necessary. Fortunately, as this book will show, it is possible to minimize these costs and to increase the speed of making a change.

---

## Why does business need an architecture?

In the previous chapters, we have introduced the idea of stakeholders transacting with each other, we have demonstrated why data is important, and we have shown how transactions fit with the contemporary Service Design approach with its emphasis on the customer perspective. Now let's have a look at a more internal perspective, the architecture of a business.

Most people have an idea of what building architects do and why, but business architects? What on earth do they do? Nowadays there is a confusing array of architects involved in business information systems, with job titles that poorly describe what they do. We have data architects, information architects, IT architects, solution architects, security architects, process architects, enterprise architects, and – most importantly for this discussion – business architects. Their job is somewhat difficult to comprehend – indeed, many businesses think they don't need a business architect. Sadly, many architects think their job is nothing more than setting standards and rules which they then enforce rather stridently. These are the kinds of architects that Emily's colleagues have encountered in the past.

This chapter offers an introduction to the role of the business architect and how they can help you.

Once she understands what they do, Emily realizes that the business architect is her new best friend and their relationship doesn't have to be antagonistic. Emily learns that good business architects bridge the gap that often resides between the strategy that the organization's leaders want to pursue, and the everyday systems and processes that are the engine room of the business. When this gap is neither recognized nor filled, change initiatives can go badly awry and the resulting systems and processes are misaligned with the strategic intent. Strategy is often poorly communicated, and staff are disengaged with it.

Business architects expose the chaos that lurks in most businesses. The business units within an organization are often characterized as silos, isolated from other business units. A more apt term than silos is perhaps 'tribal fiefdoms'. Fiefdoms do things their own way, according to the wishes of the leader or perhaps according to the 'group think' that permeates it. Strongly siloed environments result in a sprawling shanty town of systems and processes that are unplanned and uncoordinated. This isolationist thinking prevents business units from working effectively with other units to deliver end-to-end services to their customers. It is a primary cause of inconsistent customer experience and breakdowns in service delivery. In summary, it is chaotic.

Business architects, alongside customer experience experts and service designers, can help to show how the business unit fiefdoms can work together far more effectively, by bringing transparency to the chaos. Business architects identify the building blocks of the business, and they discover how these building blocks relate to each other and to other elements of the business. The building blocks – referred to by business architects as 'capabilities' – describe *what* the business does, but not *how* it does them. When an organization has a capability, the capability enables the delivery of products and services to its customers.

> **Business Capabilities**
>
> The building blocks of an organization, its ability to do something – e.g. Financial Management, Marketing.

A simple example of a capability is a hammer and the skill to use it properly. A hammering capability is one of the building blocks of a home handyman's ability to fix things around the house. Without work to do, however, a capability lies idle – it doesn't do anything unless it is supplied with work. When you need a picture hung on the wall, the handyman's hammering capability is utilized and delivers value to the stakeholders; your partner, children, and visitors will appreciate the visual appeal and aesthetics of a well-placed picture.

A key part of a business architect's work is to analyze capabilities and to describe them accurately and unambiguously. The architect will ensure that the capabilities they define don't overlap with each other and that they each have a business unit that is responsible for its content and development.

A capability is related to many other elements of the business:

- a capability is linked to the *business units* that possess it;
- a capability is linked to the *information* that it captures and uses;
- a capability is linked to the *business processes* where it is employed;
- a capability is linked to the *business systems* that enable it; and
- a capability is linked to the *value streams* that depend on it.

As we saw in Chapter 4, a value stream is a simple map that shows how the business delivers value to its customers. There are usually four or five services to a value stream, each one delivering something of value. A customer may engage with each service separately and not necessarily in a linear order. A business builds and evolves the capabilities it needs to enable their value stream. Capabilities also link, through the value stream, to the customer touchpoints in the customer journey map. This linking shows us how a back-office capability contributes to the delivery of customer value and how it influences the customer's experience.

To illustrate one way in which capabilities are related to other elements, Figure 5-2 shows the value stream and the matching capabilities of an organization that manages events. For example, the service called "Plan and market the event" relies on two capabilities – Event Planning and Event Marketing. This simple partitioning enables us to examine each capability separately to determine whether there is anything that could be improved, so that the business delivers better value to customers at that part of the value stream.

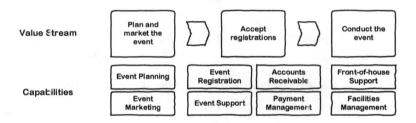

Figure 5-2 Event manager's value stream and capabilities

Once identified and described, the architect will develop rough relative measures of how 'healthy' the capability is – does it need improvement? As further information and relationships are added to this knowledge base, which is founded on a solid understanding of the capabilities, you have a business architecture that can be used in planning and deploying initiatives to make improvements.

A well-constructed, communicated, and implemented business architecture enables greater reuse of capabilities across the business. The architecture reduces duplication of capabilities by pointing out the areas where duplication currently exists – e.g. two business lines that both operate high-volume printing facilities, using different technologies, vendors, procedures, and templates. Although the two business lines consider these facilities to be different in many ways, the business architect recognizes that they are, in fact, different implementations of the same capability. The architecture identifies an opportunity to consolidate the two printing capabilities into one shared capability, thereby reducing the overall cost of operating and maintaining the facilities.

Removing the doubling up of large printing facilities is an obvious example of how sharing a capability can trim excessive costs, but duplication of capabilities exists at a micro level as well. For example, many business systems contain specific screens for decision-makers to approve various actions – approving a loan to a customer, for example. As we shall see in later chapters, it is possible to design and build a shared capability for making decisions like this, called something like 'Approvals' or 'Decision Management'. A shared Approvals capability would enable all decisions to be stored centrally, using a common data structure and a closed, identical set of decision types (e.g. Approved, Declined, Returned). This consolidation and uniformity would enable improved management information and faster implementation of new processes that reuse the shared Approvals capability.

## Business architects understand how the business works, and how well

Business architecture and service design both deliver insights on how the business delivers value to stakeholders, albeit from differing perspectives. Business architecture is a logical, internal view, whilst Service Design provides a customer experience perspective that has a more emotional basis. Both perspectives are valuable and they complement each other.

Chapter 4 explained how a business offers customer-facing services that are placed above the line of visibility in a customer journey or service blueprint. Business architecture resides below the line of visibility. Below the line, unseen by customers, lies the internal view of the value stream representing the business's intent concerning the delivery of value to stakeholders. The business realizes this strategic intent by leveraging its capabilities, perhaps enhancing the capabilities and building new capabilities over time. The associations between customer experience, services, and the business architecture are illustrated in Figure 5-3, which shows how these concepts interrelate for an event management firm.

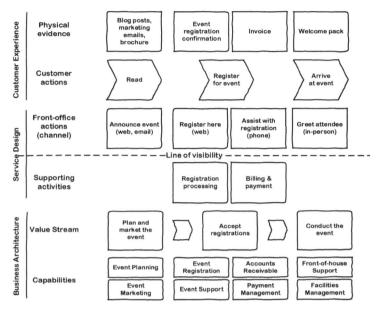

Figure 5-3 Service blueprint aligned to value stream and capabilities

The customer journey and the internal business story interlock. There is a close relationship between the customer experience design (as represented by the future service blueprint) and the business issues that may need to be resolved during the project to bring the blueprint to reality. Likewise, the potential issues at points where customers interact and transact with the business bring fresh insight to business units that currently impact these touchpoints negatively. This alignment between the customer experience design and the business architecture enables rapid translation of customer touchpoints into the business capabilities that deliver them.

Business architects develop an understanding of how the many elements of the business, from its building blocks upward, work together and consequently how the elements affect each other. Your new business architect friend is well-connected with the intent of the business leaders, and with the IT projects that deliver improvements to business systems. Your friend is an important conduit enabling the flow of consistent strategic information between business leaders, business units, and IT project teams.

Operational performance and agility are other ways in which business architecture helps a business. A key aspect of the business architect's job is to pinpoint where changes should be made that will lift performance through, for example, investment in a new system or reengineering of a business process. A good measure of business performance is what author Chris Potts terms 'structural performance ratios'.[14]

---

### Structural Performance Ratio

A ratio of two business measures which tracks how well an organization performs its purpose, e.g. revenue per dollar of operating cost; profit per completed transaction. The trend in a structural performance ratio over time indicates whether the business is getting better at what it does, or worse. It is termed 'structural' because making an improvement in the ratio often requires investment in the architecture of the business.

---

[14] Chris Potts, *RecrEAtion*, Technics Publications, 2010.

Structural performance should be more significant to senior managers than the simple and commonly-used measures of inputs and outputs, because structural performance indicates not just what the business is producing (sales per quarter, for instance) but how well it is doing that. Typically, structural performance measures are ratios of output per unit of input – e.g. a ratio such as 'sales per unit of operating cost'.

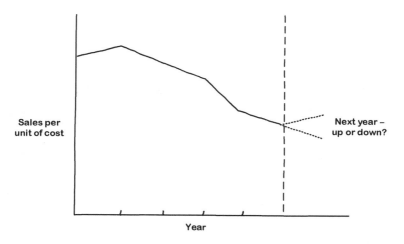

Figure 5-4 Declining structural performance

The data required to calculate these ratios can be derived from numbers found in reports such as the firm's balance sheet; therefore, complex business intelligence systems are not required to produce them. The data used is not micro-level data, so the structural performance ratios do not reflect the minor peaks and bumps that occur in normal operational processing. In contrast, structural performance ratios indicate long-term trends – i.e. they point to possible structural problems. The trend in a structural performance ratio over time gives a strong indication to managers whether the business is getting better at what it does, or worse. A worsening trend in the ratio is a clear signal that an adjustment needs to be made to the organization's architecture. This is where the business architect should be called in.

Adjustments, large or small, are made to a business's operational architecture to maintain its peak fitness. Business architects point to the places that need such adjustment – there may be many such adjustments that are evidently needed. The work of a business architect helps to prioritize the proposed initiatives by highlighting the changes that could reap the most benefit or that are necessary before a dependent adjustment can be made. There are many complexities and inter-dependencies that must be understood before any part of the operating model should be changed. This factor acts as a restraint on business agility. Business architecture, if done well, will lend agility to the business by revealing the connections between elements of the business. This enables a change to business operations to be made quickly and confidently, because the implications of the change can be readily identified and understood.

*Note*: in many organizations, the business architecture team sits within the IT function – this can cause the team to be seen by business people as part of an IT project team and therefore only interested in IT matters. Effective business architects keep themselves at arm's length from

IT. Business architects placed within IT will always be drawn towards seeing things through an IT lens. But many of an organization's building blocks are not IT-enabled, so an IT-centric view of the business is a distorted one. A good business architect will insist on being placed in a business unit separate from IT.

## How does architecture help Emily?

Armed with these tools, the business architect helps Emily to fully understand the business context of the unique transactional service that she is working on. Emily talks to the architect about how a model of the business capabilities can help her – how is it relevant to what she needs to do? The capability model seems very high-level, which might limit its usefulness to her business unit. How does being friends with the business architect in her organization help Emily with specifying the detail of an individual transaction and implementing the transaction well? We explained earlier in this chapter about reusing capabilities and minimizing redundancy – Emily wonders if this factor is the key to unlocking the value of a business capability model for a specific transaction?

The business architect should possess a solid knowledge and understanding of the many elements of the business that a transaction relies on to operate well. These business elements enable, or are affected by, a transaction, as illustrated in Figure 5-5. A wide range of elements enables transactions. These include not only the business capabilities but also the functional structure of the organization, the business systems and the data that they capture and supply to the transaction, and the infrastructure on which the systems and communications run. While all these elements enable a transaction, the way in which a transaction is designed and implemented directly affects, in turn, the quality of the customer's experience.

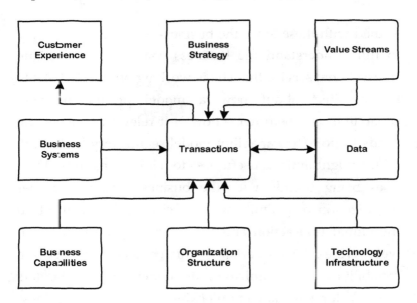

Figure 5-5 Many elements of the business enable transactions

The business elements that surround transactions are described by the architect in various architectural views of the business. Business architects create views to break down the complexity of the real business, in much the same way as building architects create drawings and specifications of viewpoints of a complex building. A building architect creates separate perspectives that look at the building from above (plan view) and the sides (elevation views), as well as drawings that represent only the structural components, another set of drawings for the plumbing components, another for the electrical wiring, and so on. The architecture of a building, even a very simple one, cannot be communicated effectively with only one of these representations. But it is important that the plumbing of the building works as a complete system, so that water entering and leaving the building is adequate as well as being controlled effectively. A plumbing blueprint is specific – it will show only the plumbing components located within the building's structure, but it will not include any detail of the structural elements, nor of the other systems in the building. So it is with businesses. Business architects, and their counterparts in the IT team, develop many views of the organization from different perspectives. Examples include the following, among others:

- a map showing the broader context of the business
- an information model
- an organization map
- a capability map, or
- an inventory of business applications.

Already in this chapter we have seen that the business capabilities – the centerpiece of a business architect's work

– enable the processing of transactions. So, a business capability model is a vital view of the business. Another important view is the business strategy (and, in government organizations, the intent of a policy or program), which provides overall guidance to the organization's work. A map of the business's value streams delivers a viewpoint of the organization's strategy from the lens of delivering value to its customers. A value stream shows how value is delivered through several services, not necessarily in a linear sequence. (Value streams were discussed in more detail in Chapter 4.)

An organization map is useful because it shows visually how the business is structured. It shows much more than the management hierarchy, as it can also show how functions are distributed across the business units and where they are located. The business units that have responsibility for certain functions perform the work needed to process transactions – Emily is a member of such a unit. Models of business processes and workflows represent how work tasks are sequenced and distributed to work teams.

Since transactions create or update master data, another helpful model shows the information created or used by the transaction. Your business architect will most likely work with abstract views of data called data subjects – these are the nouns, such as Customer and Product, that label the objects your business keeps data about. We discussed data in Chapter 2. A data architect will develop knowledge, at a more detailed level, of the specific attributes of these data subjects and design the technical storage of the data.

Using their knowledge of all these elements, Emily and the business architect work together to gain an appreciation of the business context of her transaction. Several interesting questions emerge that Emily wants to find the answers to.

- What other transactions are the neighbors of this transaction in the value stream?

- What capabilities enable this transaction?

- What other transactions and customer interactions use the same capabilities, and can we share the capabilities effectively?

- When a business function has a role to play in this transaction, what other transactions is the function involved in?

- Might there be any issues of contention between business functions over the design of this transaction, or the way the operation of it is managed?

- How will the workload of a business function be affected (reduced, increased, made easier, made harder) by the change we are thinking about making to this transaction?

This information sounds very helpful to Emily, but she worries that it might dampen the freshness of the customer experience perspective from Service Design, which had also helped her a lot. Now she is beginning to feel stuck between the business architect and the service designer – they seem to have opposing points of view. When specifying the details of a transaction, Emily certainly should refer to the service designer to ensure that the transaction design is in keeping with the service blueprint. This collaboration with the service designer helps her to retain a customer perspective when she gets down to the detailed specification of the data fields needed, the interactions that might be invoked during a transaction, how the customer might feel about those interactions, and so on. Retaining a clear view of the customer journey helps Emily to specify a better transaction, at least from the customer's point of view.

Placing emphasis solely on the customer's perspective, though, can result in a transaction design that causes a less-than-brilliant internal process journey for Emily's operations team. The IT project team, that has the job of building new system components to support a transaction, may say that the service blueprint is enough, let's get on with prototyping the user interface screens. Emily protests this approach. A service blueprint on its own does not give Emily the assurance that the existing and proposed business components are all aligned so that they properly implement the new service blueprint. The business architect restores balance by helping Emily with the internal perspective of the transaction.

A service designer (sometimes called a customer experience (CX) designer) and a business architect have different perspectives, as shown in Figure 5-6. The figure shows three major areas that must work together to deliver business services and value to customers – Presentation, Action, and Concept. At the center, Action is where the activities of the business and its stakeholders occur. The Action area contains the capabilities possessed by the business, such as the workforce, business systems, data assets, standard operating procedures, and so on. The Presentation area makes the Action layer visible to stakeholders and enables stakeholders to interact and transact with the business. Underpinning the Action layer, the Concept area abstracts the key concepts of the business – the operating model, the data subjects, the value streams, the strategic intent.

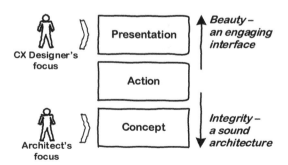

Figure 5-6 Customer experience design must penetrate more deeply than presentation, and architecture must consider the customer's perspective

A great solution needs each of the three layers to be individually great – an easy-to-use and engaging Presentation layer, and an effective and efficient Action layer, underpinned by a sound and durable architecture in the Concept layer. Many customer experience designers work only with the presentation aspect of a service, while many architects spend all their time working only with the abstract concepts. While the attractiveness and beauty that results from good presentation design are important, so too is the integrity that results from getting the fundamental concepts, and their interplay, just right. The deeper a designer can penetrate beneath the Presentation into the Action and Concept layers, the more integrated the solution. Likewise, great architects penetrate upwards to give attention to the Action and Presentation areas that lesser architects consider to be merely superficial.

Competent service and customer experience designers and business architects complement each other very effectively. Mike Clark, a leading practitioner in the service design field, summed this up well in a recent webinar: "The combination of customer experience and business architecture will enable stakeholders to design and evolve their business around the experiences of people."[15]

---

[15] https //bit.ly/2RrVWrX.

# Three key points from this chapter

- Business architects have a unique set of skills and knowledge that help to build transactional services that align with the organization's objectives and are robust and resilient.

- Transactions have dependencies on many elements of the business and a thorough understanding of all these is vital.

- Capability maps are a key foundational tool that can be used in many different ways to gain valuable perspective about the entire business, as well as about individual services.

# Further reading

Business Architecture Guild®. (2018) "The Business Architecture Quick Guide: A Brief Guide for Gamechangers". Meghan-Kiffer Press.

Clark, Mike; Whynde Kuehn; Mullins, Chalon; Spellman, Eric. (2016) "Business Architecture and the Customer Experience: A Comprehensive Approach for Turning Customer Needs into Action". Business Architecture Guild®. Retrieved from: https://bit.ly/2FPIFrW.

Mager, Birgit. (2013) "Introduction to Service Design - What is Service Design?" Service Design Network. Retrieved from: https://youtu.be/f5oP_RlU91g.

Potts, Chris (2010a) "RecrEAtion". Technics Publications.

--------------- (2010b) "Measuring the Architectural Performance of an Enterprise: Using Structural Performance Ratios to Guide Investments in Enterprise Architecture". Retrieved from: https://bit.ly/2KKgh9f.

Ulrich, William M. and Whynde, Kuehn. (2015) "Business Architecture: Dispelling Ten Common Myths"; Business Architecture Guild. Retrieved from: https://bit.ly/2E9weWa.

# PART II

# Transaction Methods

In Part I, Transaction Foundations, we introduced the idea of a pattern that most transactions conform to and discussed some related disciplines that will help business folk understand why the Transaction Pattern might help in the next system refresh or process re-engineering project.

In Part II, Transaction Methods, we go into more detail about the components of the Transaction Pattern. These include the tasks that are performed in each phase of the pattern, tasks that can be implemented once and used in different transactions, and a generic way to record and manage interactions with customers. Then we recommend a framework for conducting requirements workshops and documenting requirements.

# CHAPTER 6

# A Job to Do

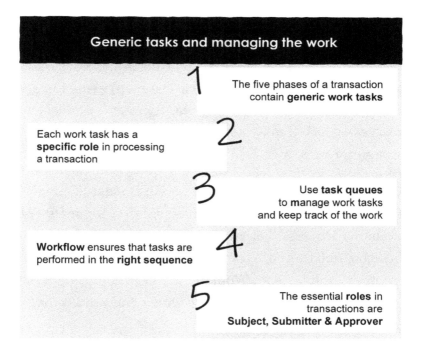

Generic tasks and managing the work

**1** The five phases of a transaction contain **generic work tasks**

Each work task has a **specific role** in processing a transaction **2**

**3** Use **task queues** to manage work tasks and keep track of the work

**Workflow** ensures that tasks are performed in the **right sequence** **4**

**5** The essential **roles** in transactions are **Subject, Submitter & Approver**

Emily has been given a huge business process diagram by a business analyst, who explains that the diagram maps the sequence of work activities that Emily's department supposedly performs. The map is a plotter-sized roll of paper with many boxes joined by branching and intersecting lines. There are lots of confusing symbols that refer to specific actions and conditions, so the business analyst has given her another sheet of paper that attempts to explain what each of the symbols means. Emily finds the definitions of the symbols just as confusing, but after looking at the map for an hour or so she begins to understand it.[16]

The business process map includes several different transactions and information services, all joined together in a complex end-to-end process. Emily finds the activities that seem to match the work involved in the transaction that she is presently working on. The map seems to be a complex and confusing way to represent a business process, which Emily had always thought of as fairly straightforward.

Part of the problem is that there is no standardization of the terms used to describe each activity on the map. For example, activities that involve some sort of validation are given a mixture of verbs such as 'validate', 'verify', 'confirm', and 'accept'. Wouldn't it be less confusing if the process map picked one of these words and used it for all those activities?

It also occurs to Emily that one kind of validation task consists of similar work to another kind of validation – the variation is only the specific data fields that need to be

---

[16] Business process maps are commonly drawn using Business Process Model and Notation (BPMN 2.0), an international standard containing about 100 symbols.

validated in the different validation tasks. Similarly, a task labeled 'Approve awarding of grant' sounds like it might be a very similar task to 'License approval', it is only what is being approved that changes. In both cases decision tasks need to be performed by a properly authorized person and the result of the task is that it is either approved or not.

Emily begins to think that there must be a simpler way to structure the business process, but she is not sure how.

---

# Getting down to work

So far in this book, we have seen how a transaction will change its status as it progresses through the request and response parts of the processing. A transaction progresses by work being performed on it, such as validating the data or sending the response to the customer. We use the generic term **task** for the work activities that are performed to process a transaction. In this chapter, we will discover how the tasks performed in each phase of a transaction can be standardized and added to our generic Transaction Pattern.

Tasks performed by people (or by machines) move a transaction from one status to another, as shown in Figure 6-1. These tasks are arranged in a predefined sequence so that the work happens in a sensible and efficient order every time. An efficient business performs the same tasks in the same order, with variations only for exceptions that cause the transaction to take a different path from the normal one.

Figure 6-1 Tasks move a transaction from one status to another

While the transaction has a specific status, only certain types of work can be performed on it – that is, the status controls what work can be performed. Some tasks are not applicable when the transaction is in a particular status. To take some obvious examples: an application cannot be evaluated before it has been submitted; an order cannot be fulfilled before it has been received and validated.

The tasks that are performed, and the sequence of those tasks, conform to a pattern that is similar for most types of request-and-response transactions. The Transaction Pattern names these tasks using generic labels. For example, the task in which the customer completes a web form is labeled 'Preparation', meaning 'preparation of the customer's request'. The same label can be applied to the equivalent task in a different transaction, such as when items are added to a shopping cart at an online retailer. 'Preparation' is also a good generic label for the task when a customer fills in the details of a transfer of funds that they want to carry out on their bank's website.

The automated digitized activity that validates the information on a web form before the customer submits it is named the 'Pre-submission Validation' task. Following submission of the customer's request, further validation may be needed that cannot be automated – this task is named 'Post-submission Validation'.

While a transaction has the Initiated status, only tasks such as entering data on a form, or adding items to an order, can be performed. Because the transaction has not yet reached the Submitted status, tasks that the business performs in the back office are not relevant at this stage. Back-office tasks include assessing the customer's request, making a decision, and notifying the customer of the decision.

The tasks that the back-office staff perform are also governed by the status of the transaction. For instance, the decision-making task – 'Approval' – can only be performed when the transaction has the Accepted status. The Transaction Pattern contains a small number of generic tasks in each phase of a request-and-response transaction. These basic rules, about what tasks can be performed when the transaction has each possible status, are illustrated in Figure 6-2, which shows all the possible tasks in every phase of the transaction.

Note that there is an implied top-down sequence of tasks within each of the five phases. The task sequencing shown is not rigid, however. There may be legitimate reasons to sequence the tasks differently in a specific transaction.

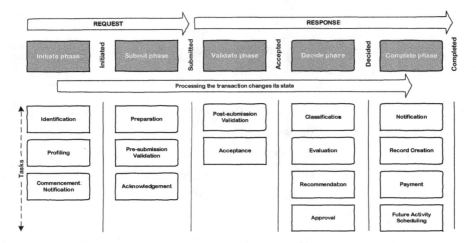

Figure 6-2 The generalized Transaction Pattern, showing the work tasks performed at each phase

In the following sections we delve into the details of the tasks in each phase of the generic Transaction Pattern. Readers may want to refer to Figure 6-2 often throughout this chapter.

## Initiate phase

The first major part of the transaction – the request – occurs in the front office of the business. In a physical front office, the Request Stage is where the customer tells the clerk at the counter what they want, for example by filling in a form or explaining their need verbally. The online channel has a virtual equivalent of this physical activity, such as a web form that is completed and submitted without any direct interaction with a clerk. There is a contemporary trend towards supporting online transactions using automated 'chatbots' and human-driven instant 'chat' features.

The most common first step when initiating a new transaction is to identify the customer who is making the request. This task is called **Identification**. This task seeks answers to questions such as:

- Who are you?
- Are you allowed to conduct this transaction?
- Do we know anything special about you already?

In some instances, such as making a complaint about a third party, the business may allow the customer to remain anonymous. In that case, a task for identifying the customer is not required. Another type of transaction may allow the customer making the request to be a representative of another person or organization. The latter party is the subject of the transaction. For example, a person lodging a tax return may be the agent for the person or organization whose tax return it is. Both the subject and the submitter of the transaction would usually be identified. We describe these so-called 'roles' later in this chapter.

In services that are made available online, a typical mechanism for identifying the submitter is to ask them to login before any processing occurs. This enables the business to retrieve the customer's details from its database and to make use of that data during the transaction, such as pre-filling a form or customizing the experience to the known preferences of the customer.

Identifying that a known customer is commencing the transaction enables the business to apply a profile to the customer, through a task called **Profiling**. Perhaps this customer is good for repeat business and we want to give them special care and privileges. Perhaps the customer is a known credit risk or is under investigation for fraud – in either case, different actions may be taken during the transaction to protect the business from risk.

Sometimes, a transaction is started by a scheduled calendar event or initiated by the business rather than the customer. An example of this kind of transaction is a social welfare body that periodically reviews their clients' continuing need to receive support. A task named **Commencement Notification** sends a correspondence to the customer notifying them to report for an interview or to submit a form with their latest details.

Once the tasks of the Initiate phase are completed – **Identification, Profiling,** and **Commencement Notification** – our transaction moves into the Initiated status, and it is ready to commence the Submit phase.

## Submit phase

The key activity of the Submit phase of a transaction is collecting the information that is needed to process the customer's request. This task is called **Preparation** and it is where the customer states what they want and provides the information the business requires. A common mechanism for this is a paper form or its online equivalent – for example, a form to open a new bank account, an order form, a driver's license application form, a birth registration form, and so on.

Frequently, form designers seize the opportunity to collect additional information on the form that is not actually needed to process the transaction. It is tempting to do this, as the data 'might be useful to have'. Often, this additional data is not used, or the quality of the data is paid little attention. The result is that the business collects extra data pointlessly and wastes the customer's time. Emily keeps a watchful eye out for people asking for extra data fields when they are unsure how the data will be used.

Once the customer's request has been prepared, some checks need to be performed to ensure that the data in the request is valid. We call this task **Pre-submission Validation**. See *Validating before processing* below for more details on validations. The final task in the Submit phase is **Acknowledgement**. This is where a notification is sent to the submitter acknowledging the receipt of a submission and typically also informing them of what happens next.

Once the tasks of the Submit phase are completed – **Preparation, Pre-submission Validation,** and **Acknowledgement** – the transaction moves into the Submitted state. This completes the customer's request and they now take a back seat in the transaction while the business responds to their request. The change to the Submitted status serves as a clear marker that separates the Request Stage of the transaction from the Response Stage.

## Validating before processing

Before allowing the transaction to move from the Request stage into the Response stage, validations are performed on the contents of the Request. The submitted data might be validated either before or after submission occurs, or perhaps both. The change of status from Initiated to Submitted occurs between these two validation activities.

Validation of the collected information prior to allowing the customer to submit their request is important for correcting any data quality issues at the source, rather than allowing poor quality data to penetrate the business. For example, this validation check is what happens when a website asks you to enter some information twice, such as your email address, twice. A similar validation occurs when a website requires you to enter only part of an address and you select the correct complete address from a list. Prior to submission, there is an opportunity to ask the customer to correct any invalid or incomplete data, and to check that the information they have entered is correct. If a customer is allowed to proceed without this validation step, data quality issues can result in inefficiencies (through the need to seek further information from the customer) and ineffective evaluation and fulfilment of the request.

This **Pre-submission Validation** activity can take two forms:

- asking the customer to review the information before finalizing the submission, and
- using business rules to validate data such as addresses and dates, and to ensure that the data presented is complete and internally consistent.

When a paper form is submitted in person, this validation activity is performed by a clerk at the front desk checking the form while the customer is present. With computerized submission systems, automated rules are built into the system to perform the necessary checks and the submitter is alerted to errors and given the opportunity to correct the data before trying again to submit the request. When the customer's request is successfully lodged with no failed validation checks, the transaction flips from the Initiated status into the Submitted status.

---

# Validate phase

The next activity that usually occurs is to perform any further validation checks that could not be performed prior to submission. An example of **Post-submission Validation** is where an attachment is required as part of the customer's request (e.g. a birth certificate in support of a passport application). **Pre-submission Validation** checks can only ensure that a document is attached, but after submission the content of the attachment needs to be viewed by a person to ensure it is the correct document. (In the in-person channel, this check would be performed by the front office clerk receiving the submission. If the service is online, the validation occurs in the back office after submission.) Post-submission validations typically require a human to do something and consequently the validation rules are difficult to automate.

If these post-submission validations fail, then the customer can be contacted to obtain further information. Otherwise, another notification may be sent to the customer to confirm that the submission has been accepted and has commenced processing. This task is called **Acceptance** and the transaction can move onto the evaluation and decision tasks of the Decide Phase – i.e. the transaction moves from the Submitted to the Accepted status.

---

# Decide phase

Once the customer's request has been accepted, it needs to be classified so that the transaction can be directed to the appropriate teams and personnel to carry out the work of processing it. This task is called **Classification**. **Classification** may be automated if suitable tools are available; otherwise, a person will be tasked with performing this job.

A simple example is an insurance company, where motor vehicle claims are directed to the motor vehicle claim team, while life claims are directed to the life claim team. Applying a refinement on this work management regime could, for example, distinguish among motor vehicle claims further, allowing them to be classified as either low-value or high-value. A high-value claim presents a greater risk to the insurer, so more attention – or attention from a more senior officer – is given to it. A low-value claim could be assessed by junior staff or even approved automatically by systems equipped with business rules and loss calculators. To perform this traffic-directing job, the **Classification** task creates the required work tasks of the Decide and Complete Phases and assigns each one to the correct team.

The next task in the Decide Phase is called **Evaluation**. Prior to making a decision on the customer's request, it may be necessary to assess the customer's submitted information against predetermined criteria. The **Evaluation** task is often where most of the work is done in processing a transaction. Some types of transactions require only a short and simple evaluation, while others may be far more complex and involve multiple people, such as an application for a home loan which is assessed (by different teams) for credit-worthiness, property value, and risk. Although such an evaluation is complex, it is helpful from a requirements perspective to think of each part as a sub-task of the **Evaluation** task. This ensures that the designers and implementers don't confuse evaluation activites with decision-making activities.

After **Evaluation**, the decision-maker performs the **Approval** task, sometimes preceded by a **Recommendation** task. These three tasks are separate because the decision-maker may be a different person to the one performing the **Evaluation** task, and there may need to be a third person involved who checks the work done in the Evaluation task. The assessor makes their evaluation, then the recommender may recommend a decision to the decision-maker. This is an often-used mechanism to separate the duties of different workers in higher-risk processes, to maintain integrity and honesty. For example, this technique is used in banks when assessing the risk and suitability of a home loan application. In the public sector and larger corporations, where decisions are always attributed to the chief executive, this mechanism is employed to constrain the number of people holding the delegation to act on behalf of the chief executive, and to ensure that someone is accountable for all decisions made. Therefore, there are often two distinct roles performing the **Evaluation** and **Approval** tasks (and a third role if a separate **Recommendation** task is required) and these work tasks must be assigned to different teams or individuals.

In the **Approval** task, the authorized decision-maker usually has two options: they make a decision based on the recommendation, or they reject it and return it for further evaluation work. In the latter case, the tasks of the Decide phase are repeated until the approver has enough information to decide. The approver's decision finishes the tasks of the Decide phase – **Classification, Evaluation, Recommendation,** and **Approval**. The transaction changes its status to Decided and moves into the Complete Phase. (Note that we use the status 'Decided' so that the transaction status is clearly distinct from the outcome of the approver's decision – the outcome should be a separate data item.)

## Complete phase

This is the point of no return – now that the decision has been made, the business must carry out all the tasks in the Complete phase that 'wrap up' the processing of the transaction. The Complete phase puts the decision into effect and we should not be able to halt these actions. If this were permitted, the effect of the decision would be incomplete. For example, there should be no choice about whether to send a letter notifying a customer that their application for a license has been approved or declined. Likewise, once an insurance claim has been approved, there is no choice about making a payment to the claimant: it must happen.

The tasks within the Complete phase often include sending a letter or other notification to the customer notifying them of the decision, a task called **Notification**. Some examples of post-decision notifications are:

- an email confirming that an order has been fulfilled and shipped;

- a letter of offer for a new home loan with the terms of the loan attached;

- a letter rejecting an insurance claim containing an explanation of the reasons for the adverse decision and any recourse that is now available to the customer if they are dissatisfied.

Since most transactions will cause a change to occur in the master data (as discussed in Chapter 2), activities in the Complete Phase usually include committing any changes of master data to the database. This task is called **Record Creation**. A decision to award a license will create a permanent record of the new license, linked to the customer's master record. A decision to change the bank account that will receive government payments, will cause the new bank account to be recorded and linked to the customer's payment schedule. A decision to approve the assessment of an insurance loss will cause the payment amount to be calculated and recorded.

If the business is required to make a payment as a result of the decision, this work is performed by the **Payment** task. The amount of the payment may or may not have been calculated prior to approval by the decision-maker. If not, the payment amount is calculated in the **Payment** task, followed by execution of the payment, perhaps through sending a message to the Accounts Payable function or creating an invoice directly in the finance system through an automated interface.

Another common action that must be performed after the decision is made is scheduling an activity that will need to occur in the future. This task is called **Future Activity Scheduling**. In the case of issuing a new license, which typically will have an expiration date, a future action will be placed in the calendar to send a reminder to the licensee one month prior to the expiration date. This **Future**

**Activity Scheduling** task is the final step of the transaction. When the reminder is sent on the scheduled date, it triggers a new transaction, perhaps called *Renew License*.

The activities that occur during the Complete phase – **Notification, Record Creation, Payment,** and **Future Activity Scheduling** – bring the transaction to a close. The transaction moves to the Completed status and no further action occurs.

---

## Like transactions, tasks also have a status

When creating and managing a work task, the team (and the workflow management system if there is one) need to know the status of the task, since the current status will determine what can or should be done with the task. Therefore, a task must always have a valid status.

The Transaction Pattern constrains task statuses to a small, well-defined set of values which must be the same for all tasks across all transactions. This approach considerably simplifies the implementation of workflow control systems and the day-to-day management of operations. The following table lists the suggested set of valid statuses for tasks. At any point in time, a task must have one of the statuses listed in Table 6-1.

Using this set of task statuses, a task moves through a prescribed sequence of statuses. There needs to be some rules about the direction of the sequence of statuses and what task status can follow another task status. For example, a task cannot reach the **In Progress** status without first being **Assigned**, and it can only move to the **Done** status from the **In Progress** status.

Table 6-1 Valid statuses for tasks

| Task Status | Meaning |
|---|---|
| **Unassigned** | The task has been created, but is not assigned to a user. |
| **Assigned** | The task has been assigned to a user for action. |
| **Cancelled** | The task has failed to reach completion, whether through failure or cancellation by a user. |
| **In Progress** | The task has been commenced. This should be set automatically when some data is saved. |
| **On Hold** | Work on the task has been suspended. This "stops the clock," pausing the recording of time taken to undertake the task. |
| **Done** | The task has been fully completed. |
| **Pending Other Tasks** | The task is waiting for the completion of another task. System generated when the task is created and there are predecessor tasks that need to be completed. |

Figure 6-3 shows an example of how a task may transition from one status to another; the lines represent the allowable transitions from one status to another. The dashed lines show the possible paths by which a task may be cancelled – obviously, a task cannot be cancelled if it is already done.

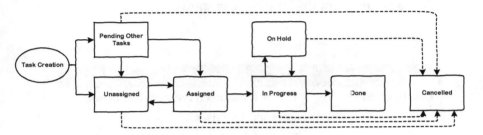

Figure 6-3 Example of allowable task state transitions

Defining the task statuses that are going to be allowed, and how tasks may transition from one status to another, are important steps to create uniformity in how work is managed. This approach will also simplify the management of work, so that work is never lost or forgotten.

## The flow of work tasks through the workplace

So far in this chapter we have discussed how each phase of the Transaction Pattern consists of a pre-defined set of generic work tasks, such as the Post-submission Validation and Acceptance tasks in the Validate phase, and how each task must have a current status so it can be tracked. Now, Emily wonders how these tasks can be distributed to the correct people to do the work. After all, she would not want an Evaluation task to be assigned to a junior staff member whose skills are limited to validating the customer's submission, not evaluating it.

Within the internal process journey, the work that team members need to perform is usually organized and routed in an orderly and repeatable way. Once one task has been completed, the transaction is passed onto another person to perform the next task. This system is commonly referred to as **workflow**. Sophisticated organizations with high volumes of operational processing often automate the business rules that control the flow of work around the teams. Sometimes a machine performs a task, but it, too, needs to be told when to do something.

The central concepts in managing work are **tasks**, **users**, and **queues**. A **task** is a discrete piece of work that is usually undertaken by a single person. Since, in digitized services at least, the customer or a third-party supplier may perform some tasks (as we described above in the section on submitting the customer's request), we use the general term **user** to refer to the people both inside and outside the business who perform tasks. Users have certain characteristics determined by their job role, their experience and competence level, and their authority to perform certain duties.

A task **queue** is a practical mechanism to link tasks with users. Queues ensure that users receive the tasks that are relevant to them. Tasks, when ready to be undertaken, are distributed to the appropriate queue to await their turn for attention, just like a queue of people at a store.

A queue is simply a list of tasks in priority order. The default order is usually 'first-in-first-out'. Priorities can be changed for any number of reasons, however, such as when a task reaches its overdue date, or the customer has requested increased urgency.

Users are attached to – made members of – one or more queues, as required by the duties of their jobs. When a user becomes a member of a queue, they can receive any tasks that have been assigned to that queue. It is common to assign responsibility for the supervision of a queue to a manager. A queue may be managed in three ways:

1. A team leader responsible for managing the tasks in the queue may assign a task to a specific user in their team – this is known as Task Assignment.

2. A user within the team may 'pick' a task they would like to perform from the team's queue – this is called Task Picking.

3. Automated queue manager software prioritizes tasks in a queue, then a member of the queue uses a 'Get Next Task' feature that allocates the highest

priority task to them – this is called Task Allocation.

These mechanisms result in a task being allocated to, or 'owned by', an individual user. The queue performs an intermediary function that avoids the need to assign tasks directly to individual users. Without queues, there is a high risk that tasks may be left 'hanging' when a user is absent from work or has been given a high workload. Whereas when queues are employed, the tasks will be picked up by whichever members of the queue are at work that day and available for new work.

Tasks, queues, users, and workflow are supported by work management capabilities built into business systems. Workflow specifies the sequencing of tasks and the skill or authorizations required to perform the task. Work management tools facilitate the movement of tasks to the most appropriate queues in the correct order, creating what is known as a 'sequence of operations'. For this discussion, it is helpful to think of a workflow or a sequence of operations as the same thing as a business process. Tasks, queues and sequenced workflow are effectively an implemented business process.

The desired workflow is designed and configured in the work management system. In operational use, a task, once created and ready to be undertaken, is routed to the appropriate queue at the appropriate time by the workflow tool. The completion of a task triggers the routing of the next task in the transaction to its appropriate queue, in the sequence prescribed by the workflow.

A task that must be performed by a specific business role, such as someone who holds a decision-making authorization, would be assigned to the specific role rather than to a queue. We could think of this case as a queue that has only one member. A person is usually assigned to an authorized role in the Human Resources system for the period they occupy the role. It is common in larger organizations to find people occupying roles temporarily. The queue management software will look up the current occupant of the role and allocate the task to them. This mechanism abstracts the role away from the actual occupant, so the business rules in the queue manager don't need to change when the occupant changes – only the data in the Human Resources system.

The Transaction Pattern encourages a disciplined approach to designing and implementing workflows, through its pre-defined task structure. The pattern defines the task that is due to be performed once a transaction has reached a certain status. For example, when a transaction moves into a Submitted state, the next task that should be performed is called Post-submission Validation (if applicable for that type of transaction). The specific work that needs to be carried out by the worker is specified by the requirements of the transaction – e.g. the business rules that must be checked to validate the contents of the customer's submitted request. All that is required to be defined in the workflow is the queue to which the Post-submission Validation task is to be sent.

If the submission passes the validation rules, then the Transaction Pattern indicates that the next action is the Acceptance task. This is a written communication sent to the submitter, if required, acknowledging that the request has been received and accepted for processing. The workflow design that needs to be specified is the queue that the Acceptance task is sent to, or – even better – the computer service that will automatically generate and dispatch the notification. (The exact wording and layout of the notification are specified in the requirements document. Chapter 9 suggests techniques and formats for constructing the transaction requirements document.)

In this way, the structure provided by the Transaction Pattern simplifies the specification of workflow requirements. The documentation of the workflow requirements will also simplify the development of test cases for testing that the workflow mechanism performs correctly once implemented.

## The data about transactions and tasks can be generalized

So far in this chapter, we have learned how transactions are processed by a generic pattern of work tasks and how those tasks are directed to the right teams. Now, we return to the matter of data, which we explored in Chapter 2. Emily remembers that master data and data about transactions are fundamentally different. Master data waits to be used or amended by a transaction – master data never changes unless a transaction does something to it. On the other hand, transaction data changes frequently while a transaction is active but then does not change at all. After a time, transaction data may have little value to the business and can be archived.

Emily understands clearly now what master data is, but she is still hazy about what information is stored in transaction data and for what kinds of things it might be used. In this chapter we have seen that a transaction generates work tasks for an operations team. So, transaction data keeps track of the processing that has occurred, and still needs to occur, during the life of the transaction. While a transaction is in progress, the users (and the systems that perform automated tasks) need to know what tasks have been done so far and what should be done next. This section describes a generic structure for holding data about transactions and the tasks that are associated with them.

There is nothing too complex about storing transaction data; therefore it can be managed in a generic structure that suits all kinds of transactions. A transaction has a status, a set of roles that various internal and external parties play during the transaction, and a collection of business tasks that do the work of processing the transaction. Transactions may optionally have one or more documents that are attached to them: the attachments could include, for example, documentary evidence supporting the customer's request (such as a birth certificate) and documents produced by the business for internal operational reasons or for notifying the customer of a decision. A model of these straightforward data concepts is shown in Figure 6-4.

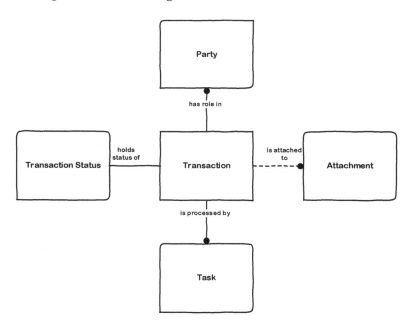

Figure 6-4 Transaction data concepts

First, let's explain the notation that we use for the diagrams in this section.[17] Figure 6-4 is called a 'business data model' and it shows the key data subjects (i.e. the 'things' about which data is stored) and how they relate to each other.[18] Data subjects help us to distinguish apples and oranges in our minds, so to speak. It is a convention to capitalize the nouns in a data model, and when you refer to the data subject in text it is also capitalized.

Each data subject is shown as a box. The lines joining the boxes indicate relationships between data subjects; relationships are labeled using a verb. When you combine the nouns in the boxes and the label of a relationship line, reading from the side closest to the relationship label, you have a complete sentence. For example, the line from Transaction Status to Transaction is read as: 'A Transaction Status holds the status of a Transaction'. The ends of lines indicate how many of the things at that end are allowed, as in: 'A Transaction is processed by at least one Task'. The dashed line indicates an optional relationship, as in: 'An Attachment may be attached to a Transaction'.

Now that we understand how to read a business data model, Figure 6-4 should be read as follows:

---

[17] The data modeling notation used here is based on a formal notation called IDEF1X. See Further Reading for resources on data modeling notations.

[18] Another term for a Business Data Model is 'Conceptual Data Model'. We prefer the former as a more meaningful term.

- A Transaction Status holds the current status of a Transaction – i.e. a Transaction will have different statuses at different times, but only one at a time;

- There may be several Parties (people or organizations) that have a role in a Transaction, and a Party may have a role in more than one Transaction (more on roles later in this chapter);

- One or more Attachments may be attached to a Transaction;

- A Transaction is processed by one or more Tasks.

Figure 6-4 shows that multiple Tasks may occur during the processing of a Transaction. Tasks also have some other data associated with them, which we illustrate in the business data model in Figure 6-5. Like transaction data, data about tasks is also fairly simple data.

A Task is described by a few data elements, including its type and status (e.g. not started, in-progress, completed), the work queue the task is assigned to, and the actual person who performed the task. The structure of task data is completely generic, since all tasks are essentially the same, just as all apples are essentially the same and can be described by a few descriptors such as color, size, and variety. It is only the content – what task, who does it – that varies between tasks.

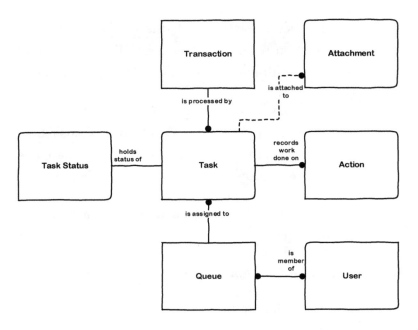

Figure 6-5 Task data concepts

Task data stores the following information:

- When was the task carried out and who carried it out
- What was the result
- Which subsequent task was triggered
- What artifacts were produced
- What structured data was created
- What documents were attached to the task

The business data model in Figure 6-5 shows that each Task has its own Task Status. An Action holds information about what a User did during the completion of a Task; for example, when the User makes notes in the system about why they did something. Queues contain lists of Tasks, while Users are members of one or more Queues. A Task may also have one or more Attachments.

The task data will hold a reference to the relevant Transaction and this will give the User quick access to the information they need to do their Task. Once the Task has been completed, the User will mark the Task as 'Done'. The Transaction holds information about the next planned Task in the sequence. When the Task is marked as 'Done', the next Task can be released to the appropriate Queue to get the next piece of work underway. In this way, the data about Transactions and Tasks can control the workflow.

You will note that Transaction and Task occur in both Figure 6-4 and Figure 6-5. The figures could have been combined into a single business data model, but we have separated them for easier explanation. Figure 6-6 shows the complete business data model for Transaction and Task data. The generic data structure described here can be built or configured into most databases and off-the-shelf business systems. If your project achieves this, the structure will facilitate easier and more accurate operational management reports.

## Bringing all these ideas together

By now, Emily is feeling confused about all the ideas we have discussed in this chapter and in Part I. She needs to see how the ideas relate to each other and how, all together, they comprise an easy-to-use framework.

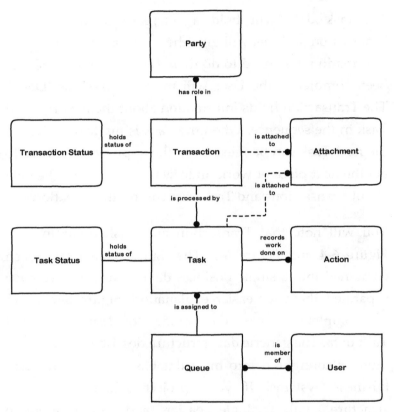

Figure 6-6 Complete Transaction and Task business data model

Figure 6-7 illustrates how the ideas that we have described so far hang together. To understand this diagram, read the text on the left from the top down, glancing at the graphics on the right as you go. The flow down the page reads like this:

- a customer initiates a transaction,
- a transaction creates tasks,

- tasks are allocated to queues,
- users in teams perform queued tasks,
- when each task is completed, the workflow moves along and the transaction's status progresses,
- until the transaction has been completed.

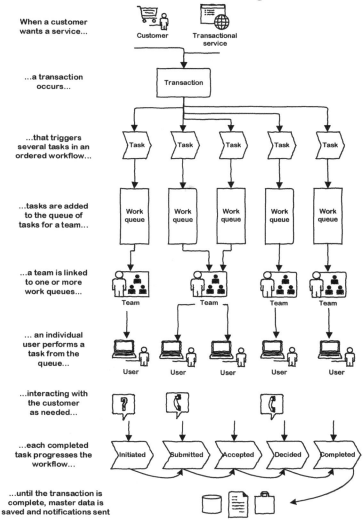

Figure 6-7 Tying together tasks, queues, and workflow

All kinds of transactions conform to the pattern shown in Figure 6-7. Efficient operations teams organize the back office along these lines, using work tasks, queues, teams, users, and status tracking. The Transaction Pattern points to a generic way in which work can be organized and – importantly – inserts two new ideas:

- Status tracking can be made uniform across all transactions and tasks, and
- The customer also performs tasks.

Emily 'gets' how these ideas are linked together to form a coherent framework. There is one final idea that we need to address in this chapter – the roles that people and organizations play in a transaction.

## Roles people play

We have discussed how two stakeholders always participate in a transaction. These stakeholders might be a customer and a business, or a business and another business, or a person and another person. As well as the two key stakeholders, several individuals may be involved in submitting and processing a transaction. These people perform the tasks that move a transaction through its sequence of states, from Initiated to Completed.

During the Request stage of the transaction, a person performs the tasks of initiating the transaction and completing the information required. In the case of the online shop example, the shopper is creating and submitting the order. However, they may be doing this on behalf of another person who will pay for the items and own them. We could call these roles 'the buyer' and 'the payer'.

When registering the birth of a child, a parent is informing the registrar about the birth of a third party, the baby. The parent is playing an active role in the transaction. The child – who is the subject of the transaction – has a role as well, albeit a passive one. In some circumstances, a person who is not the child's parent may register the birth. Since this is possible, it would create difficulty if we labeled the role as 'the parent'. A more generic way to name the roles of the parent and the child is as 'the informant' and 'the subject' respectively. In this way, the child, the parent and the informant can all be different people.

When applying for a permit to operate a restaurant, the person providing the information for the application might be one of the operators of the restaurant, or an employee, or an agent of the owner. We might label these roles generically as 'the submitter' and 'the applicant'. If the application is successful, the permit will be granted to the operator – 'the applicant' – not to the individual who lodged the application – 'the submitter'. Therefore, it is important that the transaction carries information about both the applicant *and* the person that presented the application.

As these examples demonstrate, there is a wide variety of labels that we could use to name the roles that people and organizations play during a transaction. However, this variety can create problems for us when we want to look across different transactional services. For example, 'the parent' of a birth, 'the celebrant' of a marriage, and 'the funeral director' of a death are all doing something similar – that is, submitting information about a life event to the registrar of births, deaths, and marriages. If we wanted to unify our systems and processes so that they handled all three of these events, we would need to use a more generic label for the roles, such as 'the informant' or 'the submitter'.

However, a role name such as 'the informant' may not be generic enough for other transactions for which the term 'the informant' is inappropriate. For example, when a person requests a copy of their birth certificate, their role is not 'the informant', since they are not providing information to the registrar. They are submitting a request for a certified copy of information already held by the registrar.

We can generalize the names for these roles even further, so that they can be applied to any type of transaction. The generic role names that we use in the Transaction Pattern are:

- the **subject** (meaning the party who the transaction is about)

- the **submitter** (meaning the person that initiated and lodged the transaction)

- the **responsible party** (meaning the person or organization who carries responsibility for the affairs of the subject, if applicable).

When ordering goods from an online shop, the submitter is likely to be the same person as the subject. When registering a birth, the submitter might be a midwife, the parent is the responsible party, while the subject is the new baby. In registering a new company, the subject is the company itself, while the submitter might be a director or an office assistant. When applying for a disability pension, the subject is the person with disability, the submitter is whoever submits the application (possibly the person's parent, caregiver, or legal guardian), and the responsible party would be the subject's parent or legal guardian, if the subject cannot manage their own affairs.

A final role to consider is called the **approver**. It is often important to record the name of the person that performed the Approval task. The reasons for recording the approver's name include a desire to show accountability for decisions. The person assigned the approver role must hold the decision-making power associated with this type of transaction. For example, if the transaction concerns the payment of money, the person who holds the approver role needs to have the appropriate level of spending delegation.

The names of the subject, the submitter, the responsible party (if applicable), and the approver are held in the data about the transaction. These four names are Parties that have a role in the transaction and therefore – recalling the business data model we saw in Figure 6-6 – a Transaction may have four Parties associated with it.

---

## Three key points from this chapter

- The Transaction Pattern includes sixteen generic work tasks which are undertaken during the five phases of a transaction.

- The key concepts in managing work are Tasks, Users, and Queues. A task is placed on a queue, at which point a user can be allocated to the task because they are a member of the queue. The queue is an intermediary that avoids the need to assign tasks directly to people. Orchestrated workflows control the movement and assignment of tasks to queues.

- The essential roles associated with most transactions are Subject, Submitter, Responsible

Party, and Approver – these roles are always named individuals or organizations.

---

## Further reading

Ambler, Scott, (2018) "Data Modelling 101". Retrieved from: https://bit.ly/2KNUVYG.

Simsion, Graeme & Graham Witt. (2006) "Data Modeling Essentials", 3rd Edition. Morgan Kaufmann.

*Workflow,* in Wikipedia. Retrieved from https://bit.ly/2fnUeGK.

# A Task Shared is a Task Halved

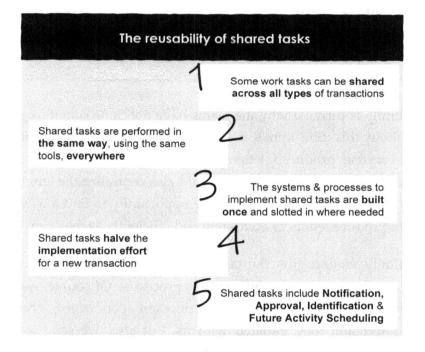

**The reusability of shared tasks**

1 — Some work tasks can be **shared across all types** of transactions

2 — Shared tasks are performed in **the same way**, using the same tools, **everywhere**

3 — The systems & processes to implement shared tasks are **built once** and slotted in where needed

4 — Shared tasks **halve** the **implementation effort** for a new transaction

5 — Shared tasks include **Notification, Approval, Identification & Future Activity Scheduling**

Emily has noticed that one team does their letters to customers slightly differently than another team. The customers probably don't notice this variation, as they get letters from us so infrequently and the differences are fairly cosmetic. But the methods that are used to generate and dispatch the letters are different across all the teams within Emily's department. Not only are the processing methods different, but they use different technology tools. One team creates each letter individually in Microsoft Word®, copying a letter previously sent to another customer, and inserting the correct customer's name and address into the document – this is labor intensive and needs several people. Another team has a collection of templates that provide a 'fill-in-the-blanks' starting point, while another team that sends a high volume of letters uses a software tool that inserts customer-specific data into a predeveloped template.

Emily is puzzled why the teams have not done something about this. She thinks it would be quicker and easier if everyone produced letters using the same method and technology. The department could also centralize the letter creation team and give them the opportunity to find a way to produce letters as accurately and efficiently as they can.

Emily realizes that the task of sending a letter[19] is used several times across the business processes. Of course, we notify a customer of our decision concerning the transaction they initiated with us. But also, we send an acknowledgement that we have received their request after they have submitted it. And we sometimes send

---

[19] We use the term 'letter' or 'notification' to refer to any type of written correspondence irrespective of the channel used to send it – i.e. paper, email, text message, instant message, or digital inbox.

letters requesting further information from the submitter. When a renewal action is nearly due, we send a letter to the customer as a reminder that we have commenced the renewal process and they will need to provide some information. Despite the variety of these uses, in the end, they are all just letters. The only variations are the standard text relating to the context of the transaction in hand, the customer's details, and other specific details of the transaction. If we had a common way to feed these inputs into a centralized team, they should be able to generate letters quickly and cheaply.

It seems to Emily that the varied uses of letters are covered by a handful of tasks in the generic pattern, namely the Acknowledgement, Acceptance, Request for Further Information, Notification, and Commencement tasks. We could implement those five tasks by creating a single work queue (maybe called the Correspondence queue) and by creating a central team whose staff would all be members of the Correspondence queue. When a transaction needs to send a letter, the workflow would assign all the five task types listed above to the single Correspondence queue. When all types of transactions do this, the teams responsible for each transaction will not need to implement correspondence capabilities for themselves but will simply reuse the standard shared task.

Emily thinks this would be a lot more efficient as well as ensuring that letters are done properly and consistently every time.

## What tasks can be shared across transactions?

As Emily has realized, some tasks are undertaken in much the same way by most transactions – or at least, they could be. For example, correspondence is generated not only by several notification tasks in the Transaction Pattern, but also by most types of transactions. All these correspondence-related tasks could be implemented into business processes and computer systems once only; and designed in such a way that the tasks know what correspondence to generate, what channel to use, and what customer and address data to feed in. A further step up in efficiency and effectiveness would occur if the tasks were all carried out by a centralized correspondence team.

The generation of letters and other correspondence is a rather obvious example of a task that could be shared, but there are several other shareable tasks that we can identify in the Transaction Pattern. These include Identification, Approval, Payment, and Future Activity Scheduling. Later in this chapter we will look in detail at why and how these tasks can be performed in the same way for most types of transactions.

The infrastructure to implement shared tasks can be built once and made available to all types of transactions. However, some tasks will always remain specifically designed for a single type of transaction. We refer to these non-shared tasks as 'transaction-specific tasks'. For example, the design of an Evaluation task is always specific to the type of transaction, as there will be different data to be evaluated and added to, different business rules to be applied and so on. This means that the Evaluation task needs to be designed and built uniquely for each transactional service. In contrast, the Approval task is very simple – the approver makes a simple choice between approve or not-approve, and the information system records that simple choice. Of course, the approver must have access to the data of the transaction, but this can be presented to the approver as a link, rather than a new screen or report. This simplicity means that an Approval module can be built once and deployed to every type of transaction.

## Arrange the pattern diagram differently

Figure 7-1 rearranges the layout of the pattern that we introduced earlier to draw out the commonality more clearly. In this version, the potentially shared tasks are shown with dashed lines. The left-to-right sequencing of the tasks through the Request and Response stages is still present in this new layout, but you will notice that the shared and transaction-specific tasks alternate. We can now remove the transaction-specific tasks from the diagram, leaving the shared tasks behind, as shown in Figure 7-2.

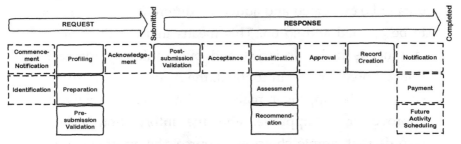

Figure 7-1 Rearranged Transaction Pattern showing shared tasks (dashed) and transaction-specific tasks (solid)

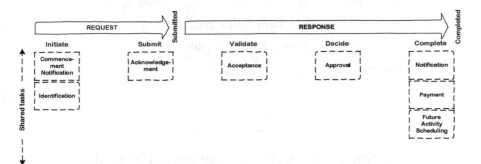

Figure 7-2 Transaction Pattern showing shared tasks only

The interesting feature of this diagram is that the shared tasks occur throughout the entire Transaction Pattern. This means that every phase of processing a transaction can benefit from making use of tasks that have already been defined and possibly implemented. The system components that support the shared tasks are also designed, built, tested, and deployed once only. Technology experts call this approach 'service-oriented architecture'. The idea is that a technology capability that performs a specific, tightly-defined function is built once and called on by other services and systems when needed.

We can see now that all the business tasks that deal with correspondence could not only be centralized through a single work queue but would also call on a single technology capability, called Correspondence Production. This would resolve the variations in practice that Emily detected not only in letter preparation, but also in technology use.

## Shared tasks interlock with transaction-specific tasks

As we have seen, the shared tasks and related system components can be designed and built once and then used wherever a transaction needs to call on them. For example, when the designers of a transaction want to send an acknowledgement of the customer's submission at the end of the request phase, the workflow will be designed to make use of the shared Acknowledgement task, rather than requiring a special task to be designed just for that transaction.

The business expert does not need to be concerned with the internal workings of the shared Acknowledgement task. They simply need to specify the data and content required for the acknowledgement letter, and which work queue the task should be sent to. This reduces the work involved in specifying the business requirements. (If the sending of outbound notifications is a centralized function, then there need only be one work queue making the job of the designer even easier.)

A similar simplification applies to all the shared tasks, including Identification, Approval, Payment, etc. We can regard each as a 'black box', the internal workings of which are invisible to the business requirements analyst. The analyst needs to understand only what the 'black box' will produce, and provide the inputs it requires.

You will note that specifying the inputs for each shared task is considerably less work than specifying the entire workings of every task. Making use of this commonality delivers a gain in productivity for the development team. There is a trade-off, however, and this is that the analyst and the business experts must be happy to accept the shared tasks as designed and built. When a business team begins to think that they have a special need that is slightly different to the built shared task, then the gain in faster implementation will be lost, and investment will have to be spent on implementing the special needs. Often, a perceived 'special' need is only a reflection of how things are done now, and perhaps an unwillingness to change. The benefits of sharing a task will usually be seen to outweigh the loss of a special requirement. A genuine special need should be designed into the shared task, so that other services can use it if they need, rather than keeping the task separate and unique to one transaction. So far, we have seen that shared tasks can reduce the work of specifying business requirements for some tasks. This means that service designers and business analysts can spend more of their limited time on specifying the tasks that are specific to the transaction they are designing. When designed within this framework of shared tasks, the transaction-specific requirements will slot in between the existing design of the shared tasks, like a key in a lock as illustrated in Figure 7-3.

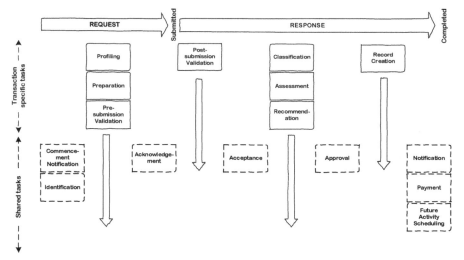

Figure 7-3 Transaction-specific tasks slot between the pre-built shared tasks

This slotting together means that when the business offers two or more transactional services to the market (most businesses offer several services) they can focus design efforts on the transaction-specific tasks for each service. Once the shared tasks have been designed and built, the design team for a new or redesigned transaction specifies the requirements for the transaction-specific tasks, knowing they will slot nicely together with the existing shared tasks. For example, in the case of an insurance company, the 'Buy Insurance Policy' transaction and the 'Claim for a Loss' transaction will make use of the same set of shared tasks. Despite the two transactions being vastly different in the data and the processing required, they can share tasks such as the Approval and Notification tasks. This is illustrated in Figure 7-4.

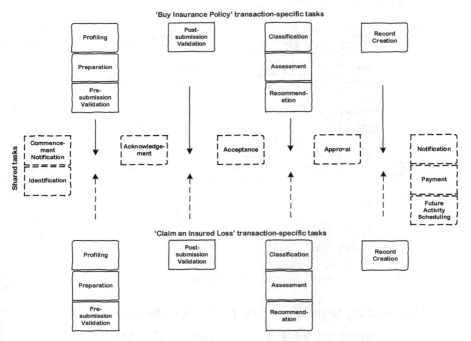

Figure 7-4 Focus on designing the transaction-specific tasks

Now that we understand the advantages of designing and building shared tasks that can be used by multiple transactional services, in the next section we will look at the features that are typically encountered in the shared tasks.

## Specification of requirements for shared tasks

This section discusses each of the shared tasks that we have identified above in more detail.

Figure 7-5 gives an overview of the typical inputs required by each of the shared tasks. This figure is followed by the details of each shared task, its function, key features, and data inputs and outputs.

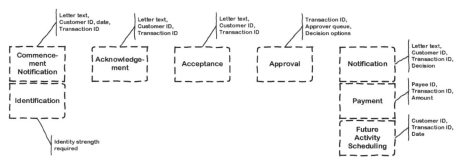

Figure 7-5 Typical inputs needed by shared tasks

The inputs and outputs are used by the business analyst involved in designing a specific transaction. The analyst needs to specify the data inputs for a shared task that will instruct the shared task to behave in a certain way or provide data that is used by the shared task to produce the outputs. The outputs of a shared task are the data and artifacts produced by the task. This information is used by the analyst to ensure that the outputs are stored or utilized by the transaction-specific tasks. Here is how to use the tables of Data Inputs and Outputs that are included in the details about each shared task:

- **Data Inputs** – lists the items that you should specify when you are documenting the business requirements for a specific transaction. Each data input will be either a fixed value (e.g. in the Identification task, the required strength of proof of identity is 'Level 4'), or a data item that has been collected earlier in the transaction or linked to it (e.g. for a Notification task, the addressee and their address is retrieved from the customer master data.)

- **Data Outputs** – lists the data items that are produced by the shared task and are available to later tasks in the transaction. You need to specify what is to be done with each of these data outputs. The data outputs may be stored somewhere or fed directly into the subsequent task in the transaction.

---

# Identification

It is necessary to identify the customer at the commencement of just about any transaction – you always need to know who you are dealing with. This occurs in the Identification task in the generic Transaction Pattern. There are two aspects to identification, one concerning the evidence that proves that someone is who they say they are. We are familiar with providing a certified copy of our passport or birth certificate as evidence of our identity. This is widely referred to as 'proof of identity'.

The second aspect of identification is the ongoing need to know who is interacting with the business, whether online, in-person, or by phone, on each occasion that an interaction occurs. "Could you tell me your full name and date of birth please?" is a familiar question when we interact with a business by phone. Usernames and passwords fulfil the same function in the online channel. At the business's front counter, another approach is to ask to see your driver's license or some other photo ID. The technical term for this second aspect of the Identification task is 'authentication'.

Proof of identity and authentication are commonplace and are familiar to most of us as users of various services across our dealings with businesses and government agencies. The underlying details, however, can be quite complex. There are many different forms and levels of identification, and these need to be appropriate for the type of transaction and the level of risk associated with it.

Whilst an online retailer might not care whether a purchaser gives their correct name or not, they will be more interested in whether the payment card is being used legitimately, and if the customer has supplied the correct address to which the goods will be sent. A bank, on the other hand, will take considerable care to authenticate an online user or a person presenting at a branch counter, before allowing them to conduct transactions using a customer's account. Government agencies and many other businesses need to identify their customer confidently to ensure that entitlements, permits, and especially payments are not claimed fraudulently. Privacy law in many jurisdictions now requires businesses to guard access to people's personal information; this requires a robust yet efficient process for identifying a customer at every service interaction point.

Identification, when supported by robust technical capabilities, can be fully automated for online interactions, and partially automated for phone and in-person interactions. Given this ability to automate, Identification is an obvious candidate to be shared across many services. It would be silly for a company to provide separate mechanisms for validating an online user's identity for every different transactional service. That would drive the customers mad with frustration as they grapple with the varying user experience.

Websites usually have a login facility that enables the online user to say who they are. However, it is easy to pretend to be someone else in the online world. All you need is another person's login details – the website won't know if the user actually is the person whose login details are being used. Since it could be anyone – or anything – logging into the site, most websites that require authentication will link the user's login to a master record of an actual person.

Websites offering low-risk transactions usually place the onus of keeping the login details secure onto the customer. However, sites that provide higher-risk transactions (such as high-value payments or lodging a tax return) will employ an extra layer of protection to provide greater confidence that the online user is who they say they are. This extra layer may consist of a mechanism like sending a verification code to a mobile phone number; only the person who has the mobile phone can obtain the special code.[20]

Public sector agencies are increasingly relying on national governments to provide a common platform for identity services, through which people and organizations can identify themselves and use legally binding digital signatures. For example, the government in Australia is developing a digital identity service so that citizens and businesses can prove who they are once only, then use that digital identity whenever they request a government service. Furthermore, the digital identity service will be

---

[20] Additional security measures such as this are seldom able to reduce the security risk to zero. Security in the online world is a complex business; a security specialist should always be consulted.

'federated', meaning that customers are free to choose between identifying themselves with the government identity provider or with a private sector provider such as a bank. [21] The Indian government has a long-running program to put in place a similar identity system on a much greater scale.[22]

The online authentication described above is fully automated and computers can do it reliably if the right security protections are in place. The same principle of 'build it once' applies to proof of identity processes that may require some human interaction and manual verification. For example, a government agency delivering welfare benefits to citizens in need must ensure that the person claiming a benefit is fully identified. This will enable the agency to ensure that the customer cannot claim the benefit more than once and to obtain information about the customer from third parties. Irrespective of the type of benefit being claimed, the agency will require the customer to provide evidence of their identity to a suitable standard.

Sometimes a person wants to transact business with you on behalf of someone else. This can occur, for example, when a parent applies for access to a government program on behalf of their child with disability. This also occurs

---

[21] https://bit.ly/2DYOKAp.

[22] https://mck.co/2Aqx8t8.

when a clerk transacts on behalf of their organization. In this case, you may want to identify the submitter as well as the person (or organization) that is the subject of the transaction and ensure the submitter is properly authorized to act on behalf of the subject.

Call centers engage in a scripted conversation with a caller, with the aim of confirming (or at least reducing the risk) that the caller is who they say they are. Questions such as "Could you tell me your full name and date of birth please?" and "Can you confirm your address please?" are familiar to most of us who have ever contacted a call center. What the call center operator is completing is the Identification task. In most call centers, the script for confirming the identity of the caller is identical for every type of transaction that the caller may wish to do. That is, the call center has implemented the Identification task so that it can be shared by all transaction types.

Every new transaction and interaction with the customer may require a new Identification task – i.e. the identification script or the online user authentication is repeated. Thus, Identification is truly a shared task, built and implemented once and reused in many places.

A common variation that occurs between identification processes is the 'strength' of the authentication or proof of identity that is most appropriate for the current transaction. Some types of transactions require the business to be more certain of the customer's identity than

222 • EMILY'S REBELLION

others. The strength of identification that is required modifies how the Identification task is performed. Typically, the business will implement methods for two or three levels of identification strength, and choose which strength is appropriate for each of the transactional services they offer and for each type of customer interaction.

Identification is largely a self-contained function that does not require the designer to specify inputs. The only factor the designer must consider is the required strength of the identification. The required strength is relevant to both once-off proof of identity and to ongoing authentication.

| Identification task | |
|---|---|
| **Data Inputs** | **Data Outputs** |
| Strength of proof of identity | Evidence of identity confirmed |
| Strength of authentication | Credentials authenticated |
| Customer attributes | Customer reference |

# Notification tasks

Notifications are written correspondence from the business to a customer. Notifications may be sent to any of the parties who have a role in the transaction. These include:

- The subject of the transaction
- The submitter
- The responsible party (if there is one)

- An internal business unit that has flagged an interest in being informed of any instances when a particular customer transacts (e.g. an internal investigation team that is gathering evidence of suspected fraud).

Correspondence with a customer is created by several tasks: Acknowledgement, Acceptance, Notification, and Commencement Notification. As noted previously, these tasks can all rely on a single implementation of a correspondence function that contains comprehensive features to deal with all channels and correspondence types.

An outbound notification could be sent via mail, email, or web channels, according to the customer's preference. It could also take the form of an on-screen confirmation that an action has been successfully completed, with an option to print the confirmation or have it emailed.

| All Notification tasks | |
|---|---|
| **Data Inputs** | **Data Outputs** |
| Addressee | Dispatch date |
| Address (postal, email) | Copy of notification for record-keeping |
| Transaction reference | |
| Subject of transaction (if not the addressee) | |
| Notification date | |
| Template and fixed content reference | |
| Channel for dispatch | |

Notification tasks employ several customer interaction capabilities to deliver a notification. These are examined in detail in Chapter 8.

A shared, generalized Notification task can be employed for all outgoing correspondence, whether there is a centralized correspondence team or not. To cater to a distributed correspondence function, work queues will need to be set up for each team, so that a team's work is not mixed up with the work of other teams.

---

# Payment

An outgoing payment is required for some types of transactions, such as processing a received invoice and issuing the payment of a grant or benefit. Payments are easy to standardize and are often centralized in a function called 'accounts payable'. Also, payments can be easily automated, through electronic funds transfer and computerized interfaces to the banking system. These systems have been well-established for many years and perform reliably, processing huge volumes of financial transactions every minute.

The Payment task needs to be fed precise data about the payee, the bank account, the amount to be paid, the date to be paid, and the accounting details for posting the payment to the correct place in the financial ledger. When supplied with these few data fields, the Payment task can do its job very efficiently, usually with no human intervention.

| Payment task | |
|---|---|
| **Data Inputs** | **Data Outputs** |
| Payee | Confirmation |
| Bank account | Payment reference |
| Payment amount | |
| Payment date | |
| Cost center | |
| General ledger code | |

The function of taking inbound payments, which includes, for example, taking a credit card payment when placing an order online and bill payments, is likewise implemented once only and then used across all transaction types. Such card payment and EFT payment functions are often outsourced to a third-party payment provider. In the Transaction Pattern, we regard inbound payments as a part of the Preparation task.

# Approval

The Approval task is the action in which someone who has the proper authority decides the outcome of the transaction. For some transaction types, Approval is a very simple task that can be implemented in automated business rules. In this case, the Approval task is carried out by a machine. On the other hand, the decision may require a person to exercise good judgement, in which case the task is assigned to a special work queue or perhaps to a specific individual. Some decisions, especially in government organizations, must be made by a person who has been delegated decision-making powers. For example, an application for a government grant may be assessed by one team, passed to another team for review and recommendation, and finally to a delegate to make the decision. This separation of duties is a key reason why the Approval task should be regarded as a different task than the Evaluation task.

In the Approval task, the approver makes a simple choice between approved and not-approved and the information system records that choice. This simplicity enables decisions for every type of transactional service to be stored in one place, through a shared approvals module. A link to the data of the transaction needs to be provided as input to the shared Approval task, so that the decision-maker can view the data, especially the data created by the Evaluation and Recommendation tasks.

| Approval task | |
|---|---|
| **Data Inputs** | **Data Outputs** |
| Transaction reference | Decision (Approved, Not Approved, Pending) |
| | Approver reference |
| | Decision date/time |

# Future activity scheduling

The final shared task, Future Activity Scheduling, creates an entry in a calendar for some future date. The purpose is to remind the business to do something that is related to the current transaction. For example, a review or a renewal may be required at a specific date. When the date of the calendar entry arrives, the business will usually send a notification to advise the customer that they are commencing a new transaction and the customer is required to do something – e.g. "your insurance is due for renewal." A central calendar of future events could easily be shared between different types of transactions. Having a shared calendar makes it simpler for the Future Activity Scheduling task to be built once and shared.

| Future Activity Scheduling task | |
|---|---|
| Data Inputs | Data Outputs |
| Customer reference | Calendar entry |
| Future activity date | |
| Future transaction type | |

# Customer interactions

Interactions between the customer and the business can occur throughout a transaction. While not a designated task in the Transaction Pattern, interactions are another well of commonality that should be drawn on. There are several types of interaction that vary according to the channel being used.

In the next chapter, we explore customer interactions and how we can standardize them across all transaction types.

---

## Three key points from this chapter

- Eight of the sixteen tasks in the Transaction Pattern can be shared by all types of transactions.

- Transaction-specific tasks slot neatly within a framework of previously-built shared tasks.

- Each shared task has a set of requirements that can be readily specified using the Transaction Pattern framework.

# CHAPTER 8

# Interacting with Customers

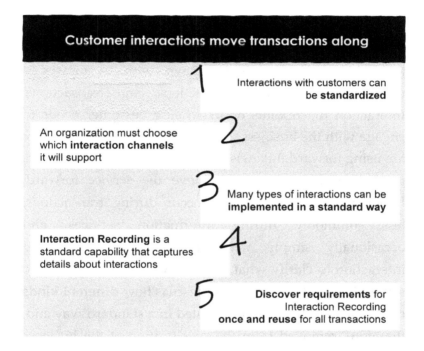

Interactions with customers are a vital part of everyday operations for any business. When you are considering the requirements of a transaction, you should be able to assume that the business has already implemented capabilities to interact with customers and third parties, and your transaction will simply use them. This is not yet the case in every organization however, and in this chapter, we discuss why it is a good idea to make sure your organization is one that does have this mechanism.

## Interactions move transactions forward

As we saw in Chapter 4, where we introduced the ideas of the Service Design approach, there are three types of touchpoints that customers have with businesses – information exchanges, interactions, and transactions. Interaction touchpoints occur when a customer needs to engage with the business in order to move the service they are using forward. Likewise, the business sometimes needs to engage the customer to move the service forward. Interactions most commonly occur during transactions, less commonly during information services, and occasionally simply when the customer needs an interaction to clarify what, how, or when they need to do something. In this chapter, we discuss how different kinds of interactions can be implemented in a standard way and, therefore, removed from the specification of the business requirements of a transaction.

The purpose of an interaction is usually to provide or obtain some facts or preferences that are specific to the customer. For example, stating the time that you prefer to travel is a key preference that a travel agent needs to know before they can offer you flight options that are close to your needs. A more complex example of an interaction occurs when a bank contacts you seeking more information about your circumstances while assessing your application for a home loan. In both cases, the transaction cannot move forward if the interaction does not occur. The interaction renews the momentum of the transaction and enables the business to respond to the customer's needs and circumstances.

As we have already suggested, the implementation of support for all kinds of interactions can be separated from the specifics of processing transactions. That is, if enough attention and investment are given to implementing interaction capabilities across the business in a standardized way, the implementation of individual transactions becomes a great deal simpler. The logic at work here is that a phone call (or any other type of interaction) is like any other phone call, except for its context and content. If the business has a need to retain the details of, or make a note about, a phone call, it can do so in a consistent and standardized way.

Customers – and many businesses – have different preferred means of interacting, and this includes channel preferences. Offering a variety of channels for interacting with the business supports the customer to engage in the manner they prefer. Channels typically offered to customers include online, phone, in-person, mail, and email. Businesses make a conscious choice regarding which channels they will offer to customers for a particular service. With the efficiencies to be gained from digital engagement with customers, many businesses are making their non-digital channels less obvious, or turning them off completely. In addition, a business will aim to meet the customer's expectations regarding the quality of the interaction – the customer expects a certain speed ("I want to get this done quickly", or "tomorrow will be fine"), respect ("he understood my situation", or "she seemed a bit judgmental"), and attention ("towards the end of our call, she remembered something I said at the beginning", or "I had to repeat that piece of information three times!"). These three factors – speed, respect, and attention – are the key measures of the quality of an interaction.

The quality of interactions has a large bearing on how a customer feels about a business. Another contributing factor is whether the customer must repeat information they have already given in previous interactions. This is a sore point when we try to resolve an issue that requires multiple interactions with the business. It is really annoying to have to repeat our story every time. Smart businesses prevent this annoyance for customers – it is also a great time-waster for the support staff – by making a record of the essential details about every interaction. At the start of a new interaction, the staff member can read through the notes about recent interactions to understand the situation quickly and avoid the customer repeating the information.

Interactions between the customer and the business can occur at many points throughout a transaction. The time at which interactions occur during the transaction is usually unpredictable, but we can be sure that every interaction, no matter when it occurs, will have similar characteristics. The content of each interaction will vary, of course, but its characteristics – the data elements in which we store the details – will be constant. The kinds of data that we need to record about an interaction include the date, the time, the customer, the operator, the channel used for the interaction, and notes of what the interaction was about and what follow-up is needed. We also need to link the interaction record to the customer's master record and link it to the relevant transaction, if there is one.

Because the characteristics of every interaction are similar, all interactions can be recorded in a standardized format in a single component of the business systems. The result is that data about all kinds of interactions, for all transactions, are stored in only one centralized set of data tables. From this single data set, the details about any interaction can be retrieved rapidly by any authorized person. This is true regardless of the channel in which it occurred or what type of transaction was involved.

The capability to do all this is usually called Interaction Recording. The standardized implementation of Interaction Recording – typically in a customer relationship management system – can be made available, through technical interfaces, to the processing systems for all types of transactions. Logging all interactions in this centralized way relieves you of the need to think much about interactions when you are specifying the requirements of a transaction – they are already taken care of, and all you need to consider is which work teams will be responsible for the interactions in this type of transaction.

---

**Interaction Recording**

A business capability that enables operational teams to make notes about who they communicated with, when, why, and a summary of what they discussed. If the communication was in writing, then a copy of the letter or email is attached. Some businesses (for example, contact centers) implement the Interaction Recording capability in a Customer Relationship Management system, while others have siloed solutions exclusive to different business teams, even when they serve the same customer base.

---

# Categories of interactions

Although the characteristics of all interactions are similar, it is useful to distinguish several categories. Each category of interaction needs different technology support, and sometimes additional data elements need to be added to the interaction record.

The categories vary somewhat according to whether they are verbal or written. Verbal interactions occur in-person or by phone and must be summarized in data. Interactions in writing can be formal correspondence, such as a letter or a completed form, or more casual and informal. Informal written interactions include 'conversations' carried out via email and online chat, and short messages sent by SMS.

A typical breakdown of interactions into categories is shown as a mind map in Figure 8-1.

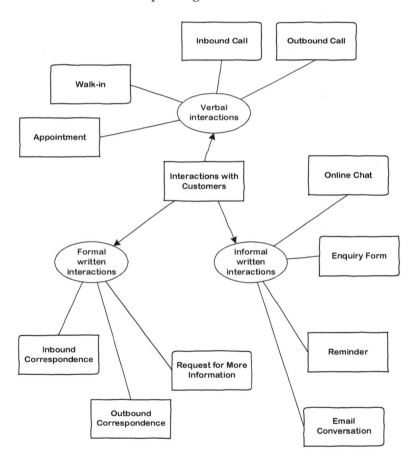

Figure 8-1 Types of verbal and written interactions

# Channels for interacting

Channels are the medium through which interactions, transactions, and information exchanges occur. That is, customers interact with businesses through channels. For example, the phone call types of interactions (Inbound Call and Outbound Call) occur through the phone channel. The telephone network that threads through the world (the channel) is neutral to the conversations that flow through it (the interactions).

Until comparatively recently, the only channels that were available were telephone, in-person, and the postal service. The variety of channels has exploded since the advent of digital channels. We now have email, SMS, web, digital inbox, mobile apps, social media, and machine-to-machine channels. New channels are continuing to emerge, such as the so-called 'internet of things' in which appliances and embedded computer chips – your exercise tracker for example – can send information to another computer.

The new, rich variety of channels is causing a similar explosion in the number of interactions that customers are having with businesses. A business must manage this explosion carefully, ensuring that interactions that occur in a digital channel, for example, do not become invisible to support staff that are used to handling only non-digital channels. Some categories of interaction are specific to one channel, while others may occur in several channels. The relevance of each category of interaction to each channel is shown in Table 8-1. An important point to note is that a business can transmit written correspondence (created by Notification tasks) to and from a customer over several different channels, and the business must decide which mechanisms they will support.

The information in Table 8-1, showing interaction categories by channel, is visually represented in Figure 8-2, that overlays the channels on to the types of interactions that we introduced in Figure 8-1.

Table 8-1 Channels applicable to each category of interaction

| Interaction category | Channel | | | | | | | |
|---|---|---|---|---|---|---|---|---|
|  | In-person | Phone | Web | Mobile App | Email | Paper | SMS | Digital inbox |
| Walk-in | ✓ |  |  |  |  |  |  |  |
| Appointment | ✓ |  |  |  |  |  |  |  |
| Inbound call |  | ✓ |  |  |  |  |  |  |
| Outbound call |  | ✓ |  |  |  |  |  |  |
| Inbound correspondence |  |  |  | ✓ | ✓ | ✓ |  |  |
| Outbound correspondence |  |  |  |  | ✓ | ✓ |  | ✓ |
| Request for more information |  |  |  |  | ✓ | ✓ |  | ✓ |
| Email conversation |  |  |  |  | ✓ |  |  |  |
| Online chat |  |  | ✓ | ✓ |  |  |  |  |
| Enquiry form |  |  | ✓ | ✓ |  |  |  |  |
| Reminder |  |  |  | ✓ | ✓ |  | ✓ |  |

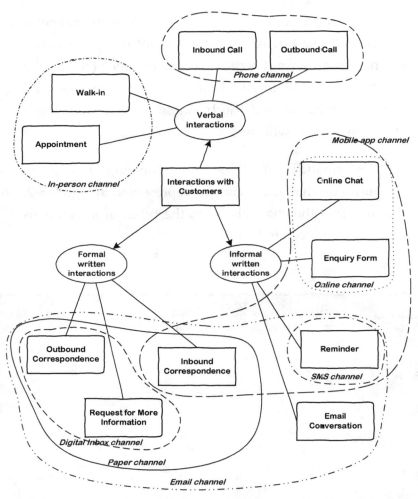

Figure 8-2 Interaction categories and the channels available to them

You will need to modify Table 8-1 and Figure 8-2 to suit your organization's needs and channel preferences. Only large organizations have the resources to support all channels and interaction categories, so it is usually necessary to eliminate some channels, and possibly some interaction categories as well. Organizations must decide which of the available channels it will support for interactions, information exchanges, and transactions – there may be a different list for each type of touchpoint. Within the constraint of the channels the business is willing to support, you can then select the interaction categories that the organization will offer, at least for your segment of the organization's business. For example, if the SMS channel is not supported, then you know that reminders must be sent by email or by mobile app only.

The following sections present a method for specifying business and data requirements for a standardized Interaction Recording capability. Firstly, the data items that should be recorded for an interaction are listed, and then we discuss the design factors that need to be considered for each category of interaction.

---

## Data about interactions

When an interaction occurs, the business will derive future value from it only if data about the interaction is recorded. Recording interactions in a standardized way, in a central repository, goes a long way to giving your customers a better experience. It also builds a record that can be used to 'replay' the interactions with a specific customer when something goes wrong, or a troublesome issue takes several interactions to resolve. The record of all interactions can also be analyzed to generate usage statistics and performance measurements. Every kind of interaction has a handful of common data items that are the necessary starting point for recording all interactions in one place. They record the essential characteristics of the interaction and link it to a customer master record. These data items are shown in Figure 8-3.

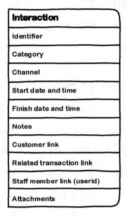

| Interaction |
|---|
| Identifier |
| Category |
| Channel |
| Start date and time |
| Finish date and time |
| Notes |
| Customer link |
| Related transaction link |
| Staff member link (userid) |
| Attachments |

Figure 8-3 Data attributes of an Interaction record

## Verbal interactions

Verbal interactions occur over the phone and in-person. Phone interactions can either be initiated by the business, or by the customer – we call these Outbound Calls and Inbound Calls, respectively. In-person verbal interactions include:

- Encounters at the front counter or shop, called Walk-ins, and

- Pre-arranged meetings at an agreed time and place, called Appointments.

Slightly different information should be recorded for each of these types of verbal interactions. For instance, it might be important to record the location of in-person interactions, since walk-ins occur at an office site and appointments in the field could occur anywhere. Conversely, the location where a phone call is made or received is often not material and not worth recording – it depends on the needs of your business. Because the interaction is verbal and not already in a written form, the data about a verbal interaction is captured through a system feature built specifically for this purpose. The business requirements for recording verbal interactions that you should consider are listed in Table 8-2.

Table 8-2 Typical requirements for Verbal Interactions

| Requirement | Description |
| --- | --- |
| **Link to customer record** | Making a record of an interaction should commence by locating the correct customer record of the calling or called person |
| **Link to transaction** | Associate the interaction to one of the customer's active transactions |
| **Record interaction notes** | Notes about a verbal interaction with a customer including the subject matter, key points or outcomes, and the time and date of a phone call, visit or message |
| **Audio Recording of a phone call** | If required, a digital audio recording of the conversation could be saved and linked to the interaction record |

## Informal written interactions

Informal written interactions occur in the electronic channels – email, web enquiry forms, online chat, and SMS messaging. Informal written interactions are rather like a verbal conversation but are already in electronic form. The organization will need to define its policy on whether to keep a record of every informal interaction. In many cases, such as in anonymous exchanges, the interaction may have no material value beyond the immediate need to impart information to a customer.

On the other hand, an email exchange with a known customer may be very material to the way that a transaction progresses, as well as providing a record of what is communicated. In the latter case, the essential information (at least) about the interaction should be recorded. If desired, the whole electronic conversation can be saved and stored with the record of the interaction.

Informal written interactions can be recorded in a similar way to verbal interactions, as outlined in Verbal Interactions above. This may be performed manually by the operator that is engaged in the interaction, or automatically by a machine after a 'conversation' has ended.

# Formal written interactions

Reliability issues can limit the suitability of delivering formal written correspondence through the informal channels discussed above (although the email channel is used increasingly to deliver notices such as order confirmations and invoices). These emails frequently contain an attachment which is the actual formal correspondence, with the email used simply as the delivery mechanism.

Formal written interactions are letters and completed paper forms, perhaps with supporting material attached. Letters that are sent by the business are called Outbound Correspondence, while letters and forms sent by the customer are called Inbound Correspondence. The direction of the correspondence makes a difference to what information needs to be stored and the business rules that apply, as described below.

## Outbound correspondence

For Outbound Correspondence (usually created by a Notification task, as discussed in Chapter 7), a letter and (if relevant) an attached supporting document are generated electronically, printed, and dispatched. For example, an insurance policy document may be attached to a personalized letter. Documents can be generated through a wide variety of mechanisms, from desktop word processors to high-volume document production machines. Irrespective of the mechanism of generation, the correspondence can be stored electronically in the Interactions record, along with the metadata about it, such as the date it was sent and the addressee.

The transmission of the generated correspondence may depend not only on the channels that the business offers, but also on the preferences of the individual customer. If the customer has expressed a preference to receive correspondence by email, for example, then the email channel should be used to send every item of correspondence.

Some organizations, such as banks and government agencies, do not regard email as a secure and reliable channel. These organizations may make an alternate delivery mechanism called a 'document library' or 'digital inbox' available. This is like email, but the correspondence and its attachments are placed in a secure location which the customer can access only after logging into the organization's website.

The business requirements for Outbound Correspondence that you should consider when developing a shared capability for your business are listed in Table 8-3.

Table 8-3 Typical requirements for Outbound Correspondence interactions

| Requirement | Description |
|---|---|
| Identify correspondence method | The identification of the method for sending an outbound correspondence, based on the type of correspondence, accessibility requirements, and customer preference. |
| Create and send printed mail | The creation, barcoding, printing, enveloping, and dispatching of letters and forms to a customer's preferred postal address. |
| Create and send email | The creation and sending of letters and forms to a customer's preferred email address. |
| Create and post document to digital inbox | The creation and sending of letters and forms to a customer's digital inbox, sending a notification by email or SMS stating, "A new document has been posted to your inbox". |
| Store correspondence | Creation, capture, maintenance, storage, retrieval and disposal of outbound data and documents in accordance with the organization's relevant recordkeeping policy. |

## Inbound correspondence

Inbound Correspondence is handled differently to Outbound Correspondence, because the direction is reversed. There are two different situations in which inbound correspondence is typically received:

- It may be associated with an active transaction, or
- It may trigger the commencement of a new transaction.

Correspondence received on paper can be scanned and saved as an electronic image. At that point, the paper correspondence can be archived. The received correspondence is then attached to an interaction record created by extracting the key data from the document, including the date the letter or form was received.

For some companies and government services, digitizing and keeping track of inbound correspondence is a massive undertaking as the volumes are so high. Examples of such high-volume handling of inbound correspondence include insurance claims processing, tax returns, financial loan applications, and government benefit applications.

The business requirements for Inbound Correspondence that you should consider when developing a shared Inbound Correspondence capability for your business are listed in Table 8-4.

Table 8-4 Inbound Correspondence interactions requirements

| Requirement | Description |
|---|---|
| **Receive postal mail or in-person delivery** | Scan an inbound paper document (e.g. letter) and store the digital image in inbound document storage. The scanned document (especially a completed form) may be converted to data through Optical Character Recognition if available. |
| **Upload document** | User-driven upload via online channel of an electronic document or image. Store in inbound document storage. |
| **Receive email** | Redirect an email sent to nominated mailboxes to inbound document storage. |
| **Extract metadata** | Extracting metadata from an Inbound Correspondence, including the following where applicable: Customer name, Customer identifier, Sender name (a person, if different from Customer), Sender address/email address/phone number, Date of receipt, Channel. |
| **Store metadata** | Storage and retrieval of metadata associated with inbound item of correspondence. |
| **Store document** | Storage, retrieval, and disposal of Inbound Correspondence documents in accordance with relevant recordkeeping policy. |
| **Associate correspondence with known customer** | Where the sender can be identified as a known customer, the inbound document and its metadata may be linked manually to the relevant customer record. |
| **Create or link transaction** | Either create a transaction for a newly received and classified Inbound Correspondence and commence the tasks in the Accept phase of the Transaction Pattern, or associate the Inbound Correspondence with an active transaction. |

## Request for more information

There is one further type of written correspondence that is a little more complex than simple outbound and inbound letters. This is the Request for More Information interaction, which always occurs within the context of an open transaction. A Request for More Information is typically required when the business cannot progress with Validation or Evaluation work tasks because the customer has not submitted enough information, or a complication in the evaluation reveals the need to obtain some further information.

A Request for More Information consists of an outbound letter, and suspension of the in-progress transaction and work task to wait for the customer's reply. The business must then wait to receive the customer's reply in order to reactivate the business task. This sequence enables the business to obtain the information it needs to progress the transaction, while also remembering where it was up to in the transaction. If the reason for the request for information is recorded, then the resumption of processing could be picked up by a different staff member to the one who handled the first part prior to suspension.

The business requirements for Request for More Information interactions that you should consider when developing a shared capability for your business are listed in Table 8-5.

Table 8-5 Typical requirements for Request for More Information interactions

| Requirement | Description |
|---|---|
| Outbound correspondence | Per the Outbound Correspondence specification above. |
| Suspend the current task | Place the task that cannot be completed into a Waiting status. The transaction itself does not need to be suspended explicitly because our transaction data model (see Figure 6-6) enables a transaction to 'know' the status of all its associated tasks. |
| Inbound correspondence | Per the Inbound Correspondence specification above. |
| No response received | If there has been no response received from the customer after a set time interval has elapsed, the Request for More Information interaction either needs to send a reminder and go to sleep again, or cancel the transaction. |
| Resume the suspended task | Link the inbound correspondence to the waiting work task. Change the status of the task from Waiting to In Progress. |

## Why is this important?

We have been discussing interactions in some detail here because we believe that the implementation of all categories of interactions can be separated entirely from the specifics of processing any transaction.

When specifying the requirements for a business transaction, you will be able to ignore any consideration of customer interactions. You will be able to assume that the business has already implemented mechanisms to interact with customers and third parties, and your transaction will simply use them as built. For example, you will not need to specify the mechanisms of generating and dispatching correspondence or making and receiving phone calls, and you won't have to specify how a record of the interaction will be stored.

It should be clear from this chapter and the previous chapter, that it is feasible to put the infrastructure in place to support sharing of common tasks between transactions and standardization of interaction recording. If this is done, then the amount of work involved in specifying business requirements for a transaction can be minimized.

We have outlined ways in which shared tasks and interactions can be standardized and implemented once only. Now we are ready to suggest in the next chapter a workshop approach to discovering and discussing the business requirements for the transaction-specific tasks.

---

## Three key points from this chapter

- The handling and recording of all kinds of interactions with customers can be standardized and managed centrally so that business analysts can assume the management of interactions is taken care of and does not need to be specified again.

- All interactions can be recorded in the same way, using a centralized Interaction Recording capability. Different operational teams will use the same facilities for recording customer interactions.

- Each category of interaction has a unique set of requirements that should be considered when implementing standardized Interaction Recording.

# CHAPTER 9

# Do we know what we want?

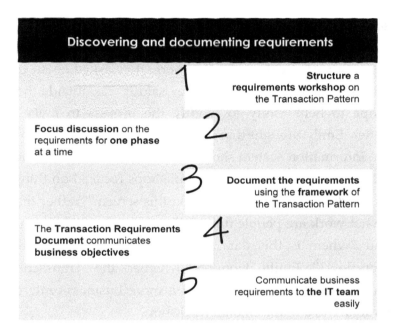

Emily is finding the Transaction Pattern an interesting concept and she can see how it might give some structure to her thinking. But she's wondering how the pattern could help with bringing some order to the random way that most of her colleagues talk about system requirements. Her experience in the past is that requirements workshops are usually conducted by a person from the IT department, often a business analyst or an architect. They always attempt to structure the workshop session around specific system functions. Also, they constrain the workshop topics to the scope of their current project or their current Agile iteration or 'sprint'.

Emily recalls that their approach always left her feeling like something was missing, that they weren't covering something important. They didn't seem all that interested in the business perspective, and what the business might be wanting to achieve. Furthermore, they asked about the current business process but they said it was outside their scope to help Emily to modify the process to make it better. Emily thought that maybe the business process and the information system should be designed alongside each other, at the same time. The workshops focused on things like "what fields do you want on this screen?" rather than "what work are people doing when they use this screen?" and "where is this data field used downstream in the workflow?" Emily wonders whether the Transaction Pattern could help with giving a more business-centered structure to a requirements workshop.

## A framework for discussing requirements

The Transaction Pattern offers a framework for thinking about how a transaction is processed. The pattern separates the customer-facing front-office (the Request stage of a transaction) from the back-office processing (the

Response), which is largely below the line of visibility in the service blueprint.

The pattern distinguishes between transaction-specific tasks and everyday shared tasks that the transaction uses without tailoring, such as Notification tasks. Using queues and tasks, the pattern defines a basis for the workflow of tasks from one team to another. By breaking down a transaction into the component parts in this way, the Transaction Pattern also provides an excellent framework for structuring requirements workshops. The workshop can be framed around the sequence of tasks through the five phases of the pattern. In this chapter, we explore how to facilitate workshops by using the Transaction Pattern as the framework.

The goal of a requirements workshop is to discover, discuss, and agree on the business requirements for a transactional service. Rather than looking at specific system features one by one like an IT-led requirements workshop, a transaction requirements workshop examines a whole transaction from beginning to end. The workshop has a secondary goal of ensuring that all key players with an interest in the transaction are 'singing from the same song sheet' – that is, everyone knows and agrees on how the business will change the way this type of transaction is processed in the future.

The output of a requirements workshop will enable a business subject matter expert or a business analyst to develop a formal specification of the business requirements for the transaction. Like the workshop, the requirements document is also structured around the Transaction Pattern. In this way, the discussions and decisions made during the workshop are translated into a formal specification that can be reviewed by those involved in the workshop and approved by the relevant business leader. This requirements document is then passed to IT architects and developers and forms the basis for system design, prototyping, and testing. The suggested workshop approach set out in this chapter can be used for two different types of workshop. The approach is appropriate for:

- Workshops in which the objective is to gather ideas for a better way to process a transaction, involving a group of participants that are representatives of the business teams involved in the transaction processing.
- Workshops involving IT and business people to discover business requirements and functional requirements for a new or enhanced system project.

A workshop, whether for process improvement or system requirements gathering, is easy to facilitate when it is structured around the five phases of the Transaction Pattern: that is, Initiate, Submit, Validate, Decide and Complete. Within each of these phases, several different questions can be used to focus and guide the discussion. Focusing on each part of the transaction in turn, is a way to constrain people's focus and to control their somewhat random expression of thoughts. This structure enables the facilitator to readily park conversations that belong in a later phase and to pull the attendees back to the present topic. More importantly, perhaps, the five-phase structure of the Transaction Pattern offers a high-level roadmap of the workshop that attendees can readily hold in their minds. The structure can be laid out beforehand by the facilitator on the walls of the meeting room so that people can easily orient themselves at any time during the workshop. They will be able to see where the workshop is going and refer to an earlier phase where a point was missed or obscured by the ensuing conversation.

Breaking the workshop into five phases in this way enables the facilitator to focus on a set of discussion topics that are specific to each phase. The discussion is centered on the tasks that are performed, who performs the tasks, and what information the tasks use and produce. In setting out the recommended workshop approach in the rest of this chapter, we suggest topics and questions that will focus the discussion and resolve issues quickly.

Using the workshop approach based on the Transaction Pattern, we have conducted successful requirements workshops for simple transactions in two hours, and for more complex transactions in one day sessions. The key to achieving this speed, while also achieving a high-quality output, is good facilitation by a workshop leader who is thoroughly familiar with the Transaction Pattern. A skilled facilitator, combined with active engagement from genuinely interested participants, is a recipe for success. Using the guidelines in this chapter, a less experienced facilitator will quickly gain confidence as the first workshop or two produce good results.

## Getting the workshop underway

The first part of a workshop will inevitably involve some education of the attendees in the structure of the Transaction Pattern and why the workshop is based on it. We have found that even people who have attended previous workshops will need a little 'bringing up to speed' with the Transaction Pattern at each workshop. It is wise to do this education within the workshop, rather than by sending out pre-workshop reading material and expecting that everyone will have understood the concepts of the Transaction Pattern. Thirty minutes or so of educational groundwork will start the workshop off nicely and set it up for a focused and engaged conversation.

## Overview of the transaction

Secondly, the workshop attendees should be made aware of any preceding Service Design work that is relevant to the transaction under discussion. This might include a presentation of the end-to-end customer journey map so that people understand the full context of the transaction and the customer's perspective of it. Also, the specific transaction could be outlined to convey the exchange of value that occurs as a result of the transaction, and where this transaction fits within a value stream.

## Stepping through the five phases

After the above introductory sections, the rest of the workshop can concentrate on each of the five phases of the Transaction Pattern, working through them from Initiate to Complete. We present below a quick overview of each phase, which can be used by the facilitator to introduce the phase, followed by some focusing questions for each work task within the phase, which the facilitator can use to stimulate the discussion.

### The Initiate phase

The Initiate phase commences a transaction by identifying the party who wants to deal with us. We may want to apply a profile of what we know about that party, such as a frequent customer status or a high-risk flag. Either of these might lead to variants in the processing steps that follow. For a transaction that is set to occur on a specific date, the party will receive a notification informing them that the transaction is commencing. The questions that can be directed to the group, for each task in the Initiate phase, are as follows:

**Identification task**
- Who is the submitter?
- Who is attempting to deal with us?
- Do they represent another person or organization?
- Is there another party that is relevant? (E.g. having a child with a disability qualifies an applicant to receive government welfare payments to caregivers.)

**Profiling task**
- Do we need to process any categories of submitter differently than others?
- Are there any risk factors we need to apply?
- How do we know if the submitter is someone known to us and special, and would that knowledge materially change the way we process their request?

If there will be no difference in processing, then there should be no Profiling task for this type of transaction. It can be conveniently dropped from further consideration.

**Commencement Notification task**
- Has the date of commencement been set by an earlier transaction?

- Should the customer be informed of the arrival of the commencement date?
- If so, what is the content of the notification that will be sent?
- Should there be any delay between sending the notification and assigning the subsequent tasks?

## The Submit phase

Now that the submitter has got the request part of the transaction underway (setting its status to Initiated), they will complete the information that tells the business what they need and the data that supports the request. For example, for an insurance claim, the Submit phase is where the claimant tells the insurer about the loss they have incurred and provides evidence to support the claim.

The questions that can be directed to the group, for each task in the Submit phase, are as follows:

### Preparation task

- What data do we need the submitter to give us?
- For each data item, where and how will we use the data in downstream processing?
- Is there any data that we don't need for processing the transaction but would be valuable for statistical or marketing purposes?
- What attachments (e.g. documents, photos, images) do we need to see?

- What consents do we need the submitter to give (e.g. use of private data, contact third parties, terms and conditions)?

**Pre-submission Validation task**
- Which data fields completed in the Preparation task could be validated automatically? Some data can be validated against reference datasets, such as addresses and postal codes.
- Are there any business rules that should be applied to the Preparation data before we allow it to be submitted?

**Acknowledgement task**
- Should we acknowledge receipt of the customer's request?
- If so, what form should the acknowledgement take – on-screen message, email, or hardcopy letter?
- Which roles need to be notified?

## The Validate phase

Now we turn to the tasks that occur within the business. Most of these tasks are invisible to the submitter, although they will receive some of the products that are produced by a couple of the tasks. Firstly, the Validate phase performs any manual checks on the submitted request to ensure that it is complete and 'process-able'. Optionally, we may send the submitter another acknowledgement here to confirm that we have accepted the request for processing.

The questions that can be directed to the workshop group, for each task in the Validate phase, are as follows:

### Post-submission Validation task

- Are there any visual checks that should be performed on the submitted data but could not be automated and performed in Pre-submission Validation?
- If we requested attachments as part of the submission, do we need to open them and check that they are correct and appropriate?
- Are there business rules that should be applied at this point to ensure that all the submitted data items are consistent with each other?

### Acceptance task

- Do we want to send the submitter an acknowledgement to say that we have validated their request and accepted it for processing?
- If so, what form should it take, formal or informal?

## The Decide phase

The submitter's request has been validated and accepted for processing, so the transaction moves into the Decide phase, in which the customer's submission is assessed and a decision is made about how the business will respond to the customer. The decision may be so straightforward that some people may think it is not even a decision: for example, a bookseller will almost always 'decide' to sell a book they have in stock to the first customer that asks for it, but in some cases, such as limited supply or regulations, the seller may make a conscious decision about going ahead with a sale. In contrast, the Decide phase may be a very complex decision-making process involving several employees, such as approving a home loan or a government grant.

Therefore, the tasks in the Decide phase will vary in complexity significantly depending on the type of transaction. The facilitator will need to adjust their approach to this phase accordingly. The questions that can be directed to the group, for each task in the Decide phase, are as follows:

## Classification task

- Do we need to direct certain types of requests into different workflows?
- Which teams or individuals perform the Evaluation task?
- Do we need a separate person or team to look at the evaluation of the customer's request and recommend a decision to the manager?
- If so, which teams and individuals perform the Recommendation task?
- Which team or individual performs the Approval task?

The answers to the above Classification questions are used to select the best work queues so that the subsequent tasks in this phase are sent to the correct teams or individuals.

### Evaluation task

- What information does the evaluator need to see or have access to?
- What new data will they create when performing the evaluation?
- Are there any supporting procedures or checklists to guide the evaluation?
- Are there rules, policies, or legislation that must be complied with when performing the evaluation?

### Recommendation task

- What information does the recommender need to view or have access to if needed?
- Is the recommendation a simple 'approve/reject', or does the recommender need to draft a detailed response to the customer, or perhaps a summary (for the benefit of the approver) of the factors that demonstrate the logic of the conclusions arrived at by the evaluator and the recommender?

### Approval task

- Who is the decision-maker or approver?
- What options do they have? Approve, not approve, re-evaluate?

- Do we want them to be able to alter the text of the decision, without sending it back to the recommender?

## The Complete phase

Now that the decision has been made, the actions in the Complete phase cannot be stopped. It is important that workshop participants remember this point when discussing the tasks in this phase. If an action that could be cancelled or omitted is discussed, then it may be that the action should have occurred prior to the Approval task, or possibly that it belongs to a different, subsequent transaction.

The questions that could be asked in the workshop, for each task in the Complete phase, are as follows:

### Notification task
- Should the customer be notified of the outcome from the Decide phase?
- If so, what form should the notification take, formal or informal?

### Record Creation task
- What new master data must be stored permanently as a record of this transaction?
- Is any existing master data updated by this transaction?

- What attachments should be stored with the record?

## Payment task

- Is a payment generated by the approval decision?
- If so, when should it be paid?
- Who is the payment paid to?
- How is the payment amount calculated?
- Are there future payments that must be scheduled (e.g. in a payment plan)?

## Future Activity Scheduling task

- Do we need to remember to do something in the future as a result of this decision?
- If so, how is the date of the future activity determined?
- Who needs to be sent reminders when the future date arrives?

---

# Wrapping up the workshop

Now that the workshop has covered all the phases and tasks that comprise the processing of the transaction, the facilitator can draw the workshop to a close. At this point, it is a good idea to outline the things that will happen next and how the workshop participants can be involved in subsequent activities.

The most important item to mention to the participants is that the transaction requirements discussed in the workshop (and possibly arranged on the walls of the room) will be properly documented in a more permanent form. This document will take the form of a specification of business requirements. The document will describe each phase of the transaction, including the detailed requirements of each task.

One of the most useful ways that workshop participants can be involved is for them to review the draft requirements document. Invite everyone to provide suggested corrections and other ideas that were missed in the workshop, such as streamlined workflow, improved customer experience, additional data fields, and new business rules.

---

## Documenting your workshop outputs in a transaction requirements document

You have now held a workshop that discovered a wide range of business requirements. The workshop participants have a good understanding of the overall design of how this type of transaction will be submitted and processed. The next step is to document these preliminary transaction requirements.

The Transaction Pattern offers an excellent framework not only for conducting the workshop, but also for documenting the requirements that emerged from the workshop as well as other inputs. Keeping this consistency between the workshop structure and the requirements document structure will help participants to relate the document content to what they remember from the workshop.

In this section, we provide an outline of a transaction requirements document. This document is an essential artifact for communicating the requirements of the transaction to business experts and IT teams. The document becomes a baseline marker that should be referred to when approaching the design of the related system components and detailed business process considerations.

A soundly constructed transaction requirements document will contain the following four chapters:

- **Introduction:** An introduction to the document, stating its purpose, intended audience, scope, and assumptions.

- **Business Overview:** An explanation of the business context of the transaction that is the topic of the document, how it relates to other transactions and information services, and the relevant customer journey or service blueprint.

- **Transaction Requirements:** A detailed specification of the business requirements for processing the transaction, organized by the five phases of the Transaction Pattern. This section comprises the bulk of the document, and details the data requirements, business rules, roles, and workflow routing for each business task.

- **Operational Requirements:** A final chapter to record any general operational requirements, such as work management, performance measures, target service levels, system levers that business can adjust without IT development, and any operational reports and visualizations that are required for effective management of the business operations.

The author of the transaction requirements document will be – ideally – a business subject matter expert, such as Emily. The expert may need assistance from a business architect or business analyst who possess the analytical skills needed to ensure that each section includes the right content at the right level of detail. Full responsibility for authorship could alternatively be allocated to the business architect or analyst – as long as they work closely with subject matter experts throughout the writing and review activities.

Although the size of a requirements document will vary considerably, as a guide an adequately detailed transaction requirements document for one transaction will be about 40-60 pages and around 5000 words. The author should be able to produce a preliminary document based on the workshop discussions in about ten days. The refining, reviewing, consulting, and approving activities may consume at least twice the time required to produce the preliminary document.

The following sections detail what should be included in each of the four chapters. Suggestions for structuring the content are also provided.

## 1. Introduction

The Introduction should briefly articulate the purpose, scope, and audience of the requirements document. The Introduction communicates in a concise manner what the document is so that readers can be sure they are reading the correct artifact and that they understand how it should be used. Typical sections to include in the Introduction are:

- Purpose – what the document is for
- Audience – who the document is for
- Scope – what the document covers and anything relevant that it does not cover (and therefore will be covered in another document)
- Key Assumptions – any strategic, operational, project, or IT related assumptions on which the rest of the document rests.

## 2. Business overview

The Business Overview chapter should position the transaction within its context. Sections to consider including in this chapter are:

- Business Context – a brief summary of the reasons that this transactional service exists and its purpose
- Customer Journey – a description and illustration of the customer journey that includes this transaction, providing a view of the context of the transaction from the customer's perspective
- Service Blueprint – a map of this transactional service, showing the customer touchpoints, channels, business functions, and capabilities, aligned to the customer journey
- Inputs and Outputs – a list of things (especially data, but also documents, money, etc.) that are fed into the transaction and a similar list of things that the transaction produces as output
- Triggers, Pre-conditions, and Post-conditions – the events or conditions that may trigger the commencement of this transaction, the conditions that must be true before the transaction can start, and the conditions that are true after the transaction is completed
- Business Data Model – a map of the business data objects that are relevant to the transaction and the relationships between the objects – e.g. Customer makes Payment; Customer places Order.

## 3. Transaction requirements

The Transaction Requirements chapter contains the substance of the document and is the largest. It details the design and business requirements of every task from Identification to Future Activity Scheduling.

This chapter should be structured to match the Transaction Pattern. That is, there is a section that corresponds to every phase, and a subsection that corresponds to every work task that is applicable to this transaction. The task subsections will be ordered in the sequence that the tasks are performed during normal operations.

Tasks from the pattern that are not applicable should be either omitted or marked 'Not Applicable' – the latter option ensures that if the task is later found to be applicable after all, the subsection for that task can be easily completed in its correct place.

The structure of the Transaction Requirements chapter will vary according to the complexity of the transaction. In Chapter 3, we discussed three styles of complexity in transactions – Direct, Workflowed, and Case styles. Here, we suggest an appropriate section structure for the common Workflowed style, which includes all five phases of the Transaction Pattern.

Transaction summary
- Narrative
- Diagram

Initiate phase
- Identification task
- Profiling task
- Commencement Notification task

Submit phase
- Preparation task
- Pre-submission Validation task
- Acknowledgement task

Validate phase
- Post-submission Validation task
- Acceptance task

Decide phase
- Classification task
- Evaluation task
- Recommendation task
- Approval task

Complete phase
- Notification task
- Record Creation task
- Payment task
- Future Activity Scheduling task

Variants
- This subsection is where the author should note any variants to the processing that apply when certain conditions exist – e.g. creating a new financial account for an existing customer may be

processed differently than creating an account for a new customer.

## Contents

Each task subsection of this chapter should contain the following information:

1. Summary of the purpose of the task and what activity occurs within it.

2. Table of the business activities that are performed in the task and each activity's business requirements. A simple example illustrates this:

| Business Activity | Business Requirement |
|---|---|
| Bank Account Validation | Validate the financial institution of the bank account against the authoritative external financial institution reference data. See business rules below. |
| Address Validation | Validate the postal address against the relevant reference dataset, such as Australia Post's Postal Address File. |
| Address Format | Addresses should be structured in compliance with *AS 4590-2006 Interchange of Client Information*. |

3. Table of the business rules that need to be implemented, either within a computer system or in manual procedure documents. For example:

| Business Rule | Treatment |
|---|---|
| **Financial institution IS listed in reference dataset** | Confirm that it is a valid financial institution;<br>Allow submission |
| **Financial institution IS NOT listed in reference dataset** | Advise user to check financial institution is correct and provide evidence, such as deposit slip;<br>Allow submission to proceed while awaiting evidence |

Because the Transaction Requirements chapter repeats these three paragraphs on task purpose, activities, and business rules for every relevant work task in the Transaction Pattern, the document can become quite large. This is especially true for transactions that require complex processing, such as workflowed and case style transactions. To assist your reader's navigation and understanding, it is worthwhile considering inserting thumbnail navigation markers, such as the examples in Figure 9-1.

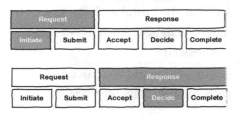

Figure 9-1 Example document navigation thumbnails

The current section of the document should be highlighted, perhaps with color or contrast (in this case grey with contrasting text), to indicate which phase of the

Transaction Pattern the section relates to. This helps the reader to position what they are reading within the broader context of the transaction.

For the Preparation and Evaluation tasks, in addition to the table of business activities, a list of the data fields that need to be displayed to the user (i.e. on a screen) should be given. An example layout follows below.

| Data Item | Optional/Mandatory | Description |
|---|---|---|
| Party Name | Mandatory. Prefilled if Business Number supplied | The name of the Person or Organization that is the subject of this transaction |
| Party Type | Mandatory | Person or Organization Type – see Party Type Values below |
| Business Number | Mandatory for Organization and Sole Trader party types | Government-issued Business Number |
| GST Status | Mandatory | Yes/No. Is the party registered for GST? |
| Birth Date | Optional. Mandatory if person is grant applicant | Only applicable if a party is a person |
| Addresses | At least one address is mandatory. | Postal, Physical, Electronic addresses |

Note that user experience research and interface design work, which would usually follow on from this requirements specification, may result in displaying different names for the data items than those shown in this table. This is a perfectly legitimate practice and is to be encouraged. The display label of a data item need not match the formal name for the data item, as defined in the data model. However, the formal names and display names should be cross-referenced to minimize ambiguity and confusion. Where a data item has a known list of values that restrict what a user may enter in a data field, these values should also be listed in a table – an example follows.

| Party Type Value | Description |
|---|---|
| **Person** | A Person is a natural person, an individual, a human being. |
| **Sole Trader** | A Sole Trader is a Person that trades, and controls and manages their business. They are legally responsible for all aspects of the business and personally responsible for debts and losses incurred in carrying on their business. They may trade under their own name, or they may operate under a separate registered Business Name. The legal contracting entity is the Person. |
| **Company** | A Company is an organization incorporated under the Corporations Act. |
| **Incorporated Association** | An Incorporated Association is an organization that has been incorporated or registered as an incorporated association under the relevant legislation in the jurisdiction in which they were formed. |

This table will provide a set of approved values, with descriptive text, needing no further discovery work during system design. The approved values can be built into a lookup table in the database.

## 4. Operational requirements

Any other requirements of the transactional service, such as service level standards, will be expressed in the Operational Requirements chapter. These are requirements or observations that are best placed separately from the task-based requirements in the previous chapter of the document. Sections that may be included in this chapter include:

- Business Levers – the factors that the business wants to be able to change without requiring IT changes, through setting switches and levers (such as business rule logic) and maintaining reference data
- Specific Operational Reports – any operational management reports and dashboards that are required that are outside of the current standard offering
- Security Controls – which users should have access to this transaction and its tasks
- Queues – the work queues that need to be set up, the mapping of tasks to the queues, and the

business functions and positions that will have
access to the queues

- Target Service Levels – the target processing
  turnaround time for the transaction, and any other
  service quality targets
- IT Non-functional Requirements – the desired
  system performance targets, such as the availability
  of online services, performance quality of systems,
  system reliability and fault-tolerance, usability and
  accessibility ratings.

---

# Reviewing and approving a transaction requirements document

Now that you have carefully documented all you know
about your transaction, it is vital that you obtain the buy-in
from your peers and managers. There must be broad
acceptance of the contents of the document, and
acceptance that implementing this new design for the
transaction is going to change the right things.

A good technique for securing buy-in and acceptance is to
hold briefing sessions with relevant business stakeholders.
These sessions step through each task, summarizing the
key details from the document.

The transaction requirements document also needs to be
formally approved by a senior manager. Their approval

gives the document a stamp of authority that is difficult for others to refute later. When seeking approval for the document, it is tempting to simply send the document to the appropriate manager, because you understand they are busy. When sent a big, technical-looking document, a busy manager will often rely on the advice of their staff in place of reading the document themselves. Even if they do read it, they are unlikely to fully understand the content or its significance, why they are being asked to approve it, or how the document will be used. A better approach is to book a brief appointment with the manager and walk them through the key points of the transaction requirements, the key changes that implementing the revised design will require, and how the approved document will be used and kept up to date. This personal, face-to-face approach is more likely to win the manager's buy-in.

Once it is approved, the document should be placed under a change control procedure. This means that updates to the requirements are controlled and considered carefully before being applied. It is not unusual to discover new requirements or improvements to existing requirements that ought to be included in the document. There should be a mechanism by which proposed changes are discussed, assessed, and approved (or rejected). If you fail to keep the document aligned with the latest thinking, there is a risk that the change will be implemented into systems and processes, and the document will no longer reflect the intent of the business.

# How is the transaction requirements document used?

Now that the transaction requirements document has been written, reviewed, and approved, what comes next? How does the document provide value to your team and to others? The completed requirements document has two primary functions:

- It is the source of truth about how the business unit intends to process this type of transaction in the future – it acts as the reference point for any disagreements and conflicts that (almost certainly) will arise as the desired changes are designed and implemented.

- It is the key tool to communicate business needs and intent to the IT teams and others (such as writers of work procedures and shopfront designers), who are involved in helping the business to implement the improvements.

Firstly, the requirements document is the source of truth when people stray from the agreed path. It acts as an invisible leash on anyone who thinks their way is better, for people's fallible memories, and for spur of the moment thoughts that have not been tested with others and may not withstand thorough analysis. Used in this way, it may seem that the document could constrain new ideas and fresh thinking too severely. This is not the intent. The document should continue to evolve, but with proper control and widespread communication of changes.

Secondly, the document serves as an effective communication tool for conversations with IT teams and other implementers. After digesting the document's contents, IT teams will turn the business requirements for the transaction into a form from which IT designers and developers can build working software. This buildable form is commonly one or more of the following types of artifact:

- A definition of each system feature that is needed to implement the transaction;

- A collection of user stories for each system feature or component;

- A target system architecture or high-level system design;

- User interface mockups and working prototypes.

With the transaction requirements document put to regular use in the above ways, the project will be well-equipped to achieve its stated objectives.

## Three key points from this chapter

- A workshop, structured on the Transaction Pattern, is an effective and manageable way to engage business staff and draw out ideas for improving a transaction.

- The workshop results in an array of ideas and definite requirements that should be documented in a formal 'transaction requirements document', which is also structured using the Transaction Pattern.

- The completed and approved transaction requirements document becomes the key tool to communicate business objectives and specific needs to IT teams and to keep your peers in the business units 'on song'.

# PART III

---

# Implementing Transactions

In Part II, Transaction Methods, we explained the components of the Transaction Pattern, including a detailed look at the tasks that are performed in each phase of the pattern. We also recommended a framework for conducting requirements workshops and documenting requirements.

In Part III, Implementing Transactions, we offer guidance on the steps that you should take when implementing the Transaction Pattern and the associated techniques we have outlined in Parts I and II. We work through a case study to illustrate how these techniques are applied in real situations. Finally, we discuss the benefits that could flow from using these techniques. We look at the immediate benefits of using each of the techniques, as well as the medium- and longer-term strategic benefits that can be achieved by using all the techniques in a coordinated program.

# CHAPTER 10

# Fomenting Revolution

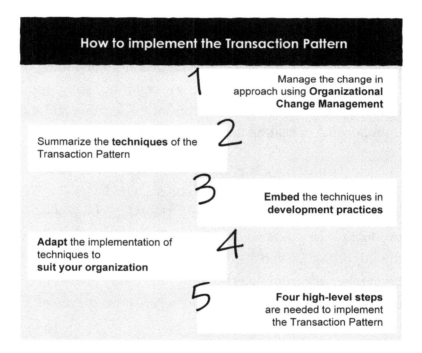

**How to implement the Transaction Pattern**

1 Manage the change in approach using **Organizational Change Management**

2 Summarize the **techniques** of the Transaction Pattern

3 **Embed** the techniques in development practices

4 **Adapt** the implementation of techniques to **suit your organization**

5 **Four high-level steps** are needed to implement the Transaction Pattern

Last night Emily read the old Aesop's fable about the tortoise and the hare to her child. The tortoise, weary of the hare's boasting about how fast he runs, challenges him to a race. The hare – overconfident in his speed – lies down for a nap, and the tortoise wins the race.

Afterwards, Emily wonders whether we really believe the fable's message. Do we behave like the tortoise, or like the hare? Which is better? We forget the lesson of the fable. In real life, we shift our focus too quickly and put our minds to sleep rather too often. This is true in business projects and large IT investments, as much as in our personal lives.

The tortoise knows what it needs to do and the pattern of work that it needs to employ to reach the finish line. The hare stops for a sleep and jumps around from one thing to another, turning its attention to anything shiny and interesting. It is easily distracted from the journey and the ultimate goal of beating the tortoise.

The hare would love the 'Agile' approach that is in favor with many software developers and system designers. The agile hares run fast in 'sprints'. They race to release a product to users – "Hey look, we have built a terrific new digital service for you!" – but it is only a partial solution, at best. Like an incomplete building, the users are allowed onto the building site too early, when only the foyer is ready for use.

Through such regular builds of software, the agile hare attests that he is making rapid progress. But in a project that is building a serious business system, the race to release the product of a few sprints achieves little except a pat on the back and a nice nap afterwards.

In Agile IT projects, the hares dance around with great energy. The latest thought or challenge easily distracts them, and they lose focus on where they are going. Although well-managed Agile IT projects will begin with an overall design and will ensure that the product of each sprint aligns with the design, we have observed that this rarely happens in practice. The holistic and enduring target design is often sidelined. Yet the hares still expect to deliver a coherent system that properly supports the business processes, while pulling their team in all directions, believing this is what being agile means.

We need a better, more tortoise-like approach. We need a method that delivers coherent, well-structured business processes and systems. This approach would build a holistic solution using proven patterns, with doggedness and persistence. We would keep the end-goal at the front of our minds – like the tortoise. The tortoise's approach would deliver a joined-up end-to-end service journey, and – more importantly – the efficient and repeatable back-office processes that fulfil the promise to the customer.

The passing fashions of the IT world serve to distract the hare from getting to the finish line: Agile development methods, scenarios, user stories, prototyping, user research, design thinking, service design, user experience design, and so on. The tortoise might use some – or all – of these techniques; there is no denying they can be useful. But he knows that producing a worthwhile business system requires much more than a shiny new tool. It requires persistence, as well as the ability to remember the goal, and make constant progress towards it. Progress is not so much about delivering some, or any, working software, but about designing and assembling all the pieces methodically in alignment with a planned target.

When constructing a building or a bridge, correcting an error in the design or adapting to a change in the client's brief can be expensive. Beyond a certain point, there is no going back. The hares in the software industry exploit the fact that developing systems is not like constructing a building or a bridge. It is much less costly to fix a mistake in software or to meet an emerging new requirement. Provided, that is, you still have some investment capital left. If the money runs out, the hares may release the product anyway so as not to 'waste' the investment.

The tortoises avoid getting into that situation by discovering the client's objective and requirements quickly. They design a robust target that links people, process, data, and technology in a seamless whole. The tortoises rely on using simple patterns to design and build the target quickly yet robustly. They insert data levers and switches that business folk can adjust down the line, without further IT investment.

Many large IT projects fail to deliver a complete product or meet the strategic objective, leaving disappointed investors and users in their wake. Poorly expressed and undiscovered business requirements are often the root cause of these failures, but only rarely are they exposed as such because people are loath to learn what to do differently next time. The fashionable hare-driven methods will probably not arrest the growth in costs and mounting failures. There is little evidence to date that the Agile methods have greatly improved project outcomes.

We need to stop sprinting and napping like the hare. The tortoise sticks to the long game. He knows where the finish line is, and he knows how to reach it. Let's behave like the tortoise.

## Managing change

Emily is excited. She loves the fresh approaches she has been learning about and enjoys working as the subject matter expert on a system redevelopment project. Basing the business requirements on the Transaction Pattern really helped the team to deliver a business system that supported an improved internal business process. The alignment between the business requirements and the desired service design enabled the development of a much-improved customer experience.

Emily is keen to keep her rebellion alive. She recognizes that persuading others to use the new approaches calls for them to accept changes in the way they do things. She has seen how difficult it can be to bring about change in the processes and the culture of her organization. Emily wonders why change is so hard.

Often, change is difficult because there is too much of it. Emily's colleagues are weary of the constant change initiatives that management foists upon them, yet that do not seem to achieve much. Managers love to tinker with easy things like the organizational structure, believing that a 'better' structure will make the organization work better. Usually though, restructures only change the responsibilities of the senior managers and their reporting lines, with no effect on how well the business works. Other management favorites include outsourcing of certain services, new computers and software, centralizing shared services, measuring staff performance, ard reversing previous change initiatives.

Everyone is aware that the pace of change is accelerating. There are many factors that drive this acceleration, not all of them management fashions. A significant driver of change is technology innovation and continuous efforts to maintain competitive advantage and save on costs. But the cumulative effect on staff of change on top of change is often great fatigue and – ironically – less efficiency and fleeting benefits. There is a growing recognition since the 1990s that programs that aim to deliver transformational change fail more often than they succeed.

The problem with change may be even more fundamental and embedded in the way businesses are designed.

According to management innovators, Gary Hamel and Michele Zanini:

> *The reality is that today's organizations were simply never designed to change proactively and deeply—they were built for discipline and efficiency, enforced through hierarchy and routinization. As a result, there's a mismatch between the pace of change in the external environment and the fastest possible pace of change at most organizations.*[23]

How can we run change initiatives that really 'stick' and make a lasting difference? Part of the answer is that we need to manage the change explicitly. This is encapsulated in a growing specialization known as Organizational Change Management. More than simply helping people to deal with changes or controlling changes to business plans or system projects, Organizational Change Management focuses broadly on what needs to change within the whole organization. It includes many different disciplines – from behavioral science to business solutions and technology.

Organizational Change Management employs a structured approach to implement change successfully with minimal disruption to business operations. The goal is to achieve lasting benefits. While many different models of change have been tried over recent decades, change managers – now a recognized vocation – have settled on a few that have been proven. Comprehensive guides to the methods

---

[23] Gary Hamel and Michele Zanini (2014).

and competencies required to manage change effectively have been developed. Including a well-trained and competent change manager in a project team is an important step towards making change 'stick'.[24]

---

## Managing the change of adopting the Transaction Pattern

While implementing the Transaction Pattern in your organization may not be on the same scale as a large transformational change initiative, some of the practices of modern Organizational Change Management will prove helpful. Implementing the Transaction Pattern might be tackled as an across-the-board change to the methods by which the organization develops systems and improves business processes. This approach would require adoption of the approaches outlined in this book by your colleagues in a wide range of disciplines. It would also require winning the support of a senior executive who would mandate the change and champion it throughout the business.

A more successful approach, however, is to just start small and gradually build a following. Emily decides on this

---

[24] Helpful resources for learning more about Change Management can be found at the end of this chapter.

option after using the Transaction Pattern in a small way for a while. Now that she has demonstrated that the techniques work, Emily thinks that other people will want to adopt it too.

In fact, implementing the Transaction Pattern has a low barrier to entry. It involves tweaking or modestly amending processes that you are already likely doing in some form. It requires no additional software tools and it can be begun within a single project.

Despite this low barrier, we have found that changing system design and development methods inevitably gives rise to objections and obstructions. Emily will need to be prepared to manage them. One way to be prepared is to be thoroughly familiar with the organization's current system development practices. This will be known as the 'System Development Life Cycle', the 'System Development Method', the 'Agile Development Method', or a similar name. Bear in mind that the current practices may not be formally documented; teams just know 'the way we do things here'. They are the set of practices that your business and IT people actually use in projects.

The standard practices, whatever they are called and whether documented or not, will most likely contain variants for different kinds of projects, such as a system refresh, a new system, process re-engineering, or introduction of a new product or service. There may even be several methods in different parts of the organization, especially in a larger organization. The system development practices will have a flavor of 'requirements up-front' (often called 'Waterfall') or 'requirements as-we-go' ('Agile'). (We outlined these two fundamental attitudes to system development in Chapter 1.) These two basic approaches have much in common. Successful proponents of both employ many of the same features. If documented, the practices will appear to be sensible and methodical – more tortoise-like than hare-like. In practice, however, sensible, methodical practices are often distorted by the pressures of reality or the whims of the participants in the project.

Slipping the Transaction Pattern techniques in between these existing practices in her current project is a low-risk way for Emily to begin her quiet rebellion and perhaps to find a few other people who want to adopt the practices. In turn, they will influence others. In this way, Emily's initial tentative actions will grow into a broad network of influencers in her business.

In the rest of this chapter, we summarize each of the techniques discussed in this book, including the business outcomes that will result from using them. We also set out four key steps to take when implementing the Transaction Pattern and its associated techniques.

# Transaction Pattern techniques

When Emily began using the techniques we have outlined in this book, she found that she needed a concise summary of each technique. All these techniques support the effective use of the Transaction Pattern in some way. We believe that using all these techniques will benefit any business improvement or system redevelopment project. However, it is not essential that all techniques be implemented at once – a gradual introduction of some techniques may be the most successful approach in a given situation. Be aware that, ultimately, you will call upon all these techniques to get the best out of the Transaction Pattern and to embed the use of the pattern successfully in your organization.

| Technique | What does this achieve? |
|---|---|
| **Business Glossary** Identify data subjects and define business terms unambiguously. | Reduced ambiguity and confusion about the meaning of terms and the organization's data assets. |
| **Service Design** Use service blueprints and other techniques of Service Design, including: user research, journey mapping, touchpoints (interactions and transactions), personas, service scenarios, design workshops. | Business model aligns to customer experience. |

| Technique | What does this achieve? |
|---|---|
| **Value Stream Mapping** Develop a high-level process map comprising 5-7 services by which value is delivered to customers. | Understanding of how the organization delivers value to stakeholders and how it intends to deliver value in the future through a different strategy. |
| **Business Capability Mapping** Develop a map of business capabilities and define each as: "The ability to …"; Map each capability to people, process, information, and technology elements. | Comprehensive understanding of what the business does; Ability to measure the health, and the planned future health, of capabilities; Ability to analyze the impact of projects. |
| **Master Data and Generalized Transaction Data** Distinguish between master data and transaction data (remember: transactions update master data); Generalize the structure of transaction data. | Improved control of master data; More accurate and cheaper management reporting on transactions. |
| **Transactions Discovery** Marry the Service Blueprint to the Transaction Pattern; Follow the master data and use a value stream map to identify transactions in the customer journey. | Clarity on what each transaction does and where it begins and ends. |

| Technique | What does this achieve? |
|---|---|
| **Standardized Transaction Processes**<br>Apply standard transaction process phases (Initiate, Submit, Validate, Decide, Complete) to replace product or organizational variations. | Reporting on performance is more accurate and easier; Customer and internal process journeys harmonized. |
| **Standardized Work Tasks**<br>Apply standardized work tasks to transaction processes; Identify and design shared tasks across transactions and transaction phases. | Customer self-service is enabled; The work involved in processing a type of transaction is segmented in a uniform way that is easily applied to a different type of transaction. |
| **Queues and Workflows Design**<br>Design user roles, workflows and task queues. | Business processes and workflows are clearly defined. |
| **Generalized Customer Interactions**<br>Design standardized generic customer interactions and channels. | Standardized implementations of customer interaction touchpoints. |
| **Business Requirements Discovery and Documenting**<br>Document business requirements and process workflows by employing the Transaction Pattern to structure requirements gathering workshop(s). | Requirements more structured and focused, customer and internal views balanced, standardization maximized, lower cost, higher reuse, agility, performance; Improved communication with IT; Simplified security and access control. |

## Steps to implementing the Transaction Pattern

In this section, we describe four key steps to take towards implementing the Transaction Pattern and the associated techniques outlined above.

| Step 1 | Review current practices |
|---|---|
| **What to do** | Review your system development method, focusing on the role of business in representing requirements in the method. |
| **Be awake to** | Bear in mind the method may not be formally documented. How are the systems specification and requirements specification and design done in your organization? |

| Step 2 | Identify gaps |
|---|---|
| **What to do** | Map the Transaction Pattern techniques against your system development method to identify gaps that will need to be addressed by change management. |
| **Be awake to** | Some techniques may be easily bridged from your current practices because they are similar. Others may require a greater stretch. These will require careful stakeholder management and a firm view of the value proposition of making the change. |

| Step 3 | Implement Transaction Pattern techniques |
|---|---|
| **What to do** | Implement key Transaction Pattern techniques by communicating the benefits, training people to help them adopt the change, providing templates and guides to make the change easier and to help ensure the consistent application of the approaches. |
| **Be awake to** | It is important to regularly emphasize why the change is necessary and the improvements that it will deliver. |

| Step 4 | Promote successes |
|---|---|
| **What to do** | Publish and celebrate successes and the realization of positive outcomes. |
| **Be awake to** | Use positive stories to enlist more supporters for Emily's rebellion. |

## Three key points from this chapter

- Ensuring that a change 'sticks' can be difficult; it needs to be managed explicitly.

- Several Transaction Pattern techniques work together and should be implemented in a sequence and pace that suits your organization.

- Four high-level activities or steps are needed to embed the use of the Transaction Pattern and to demonstrate its positive outcomes.

---

## Further reading

*ACMP's Certified Change Management Professional program;* The Association of Change Management Professionals; Retrieved from https://bit.ly/2PdtR5Q.

*Change Management,* Wikipedia, Retrieved from https://bit.ly/2AFiGxs.

Hamel, Gary and Zanini, Michele. (2014) *Build a change platform, not a change program;* McKinsey; Retrieved from https://mck.co/2xYzz2N.

# CHAPTER 11

# Putting the Pattern into Practice

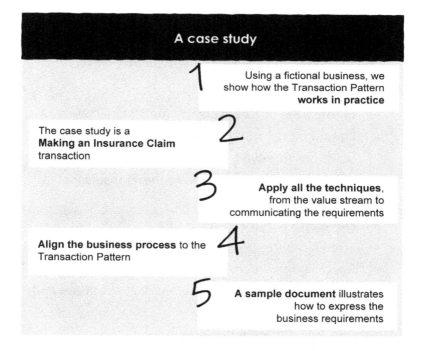

This chapter illustrates how the Transaction Pattern that we have described in Parts I and II can be put to work in practice. We work through a case study step by step, progressively building the requirements specification that will lead to implementation of the transaction in systems and work practices. Through this concrete example, we hope to illustrate how the Transaction Pattern and the associated method could be used in your own business scenarios. The case study involves a realistic but fictitious transaction. Firstly, we present an overview of the design and specification steps that are necessary for this case study. Then we delve into the details of each step in the subsequent sections. The steps involved in this case study are:

- Introduce the case study scenario
- Map the value stream
- Map the customer journey
- Identify the business objects (data subjects)
- Describe the business process and organization functions involved
- Align the business process to the Transaction Pattern
- Develop a service blueprint for the process
- Hold a requirements workshop
- Specify the sequence of tasks
- Specify the data requirements for Preparation and Evaluation
- Specify validation business rules
- Specify the workflow and work queues
- Communicate the requirements
- Discuss implementation options with IT.

Our subject matter expert, Emily, takes the lead in this case study.

# The case study scenario

The case study concerns an insurance company, Rebel Insurance, who market and sell insurance policies that protect the policyholder against losses caused by a wide range of unexpected incidents. Insurance policies are available from Rebel Insurance for everything from health expenses to death; from damage to buildings to damage to reputations; from unexpected events during travel to the sinking of ships. Like most insurers, Rebel Insurance has become adept at assessing and costing the risk of every sort of loss that individuals and organizations might suffer.

The insurance industry is huge and varied in many ways, yet there are remarkably consistent norms on which most insurers base their business model. All insurers produce policy documents that detail the risks that are covered and those that are excluded. All insurers need to process claims against a policy when the owner of the policy experiences a loss. All insurers must assess and settle every claim they receive. All insurers will seek to renew the policies with existing customers when expiration of a policy is imminent.

Insurance companies make a good topic for this case study because the processes and information that insurers typically use are well-described. In particular, the case study focuses on the transaction that most customers hope they will never need to engage with – making an insurance claim. Processing insurance claims forms the bulk of the work in Rebel Insurance's office, alongside sales of policies. Insurers are always striving to process claims more efficiently, because claims processing is a significant cost that ultimately flows through to the premiums the company charges. Higher premiums make Rebel Insurance less competitive.

## The value stream

Firstly, Emily looks at Rebel Insurance's value stream – that is, the set of services by which the insurer hopes to provide value to their policyholders.

> **Value Stream**
>
> A high-level business process map showing 5-7 key activities that deliver a product or service to customers; it communicates what the organization is in the business of doing.

Rebel Insurance develops and markets their products, underwrites and sells policies, processes claims, and renews policies. The company's value stream maps these services as a linear sequence (although the services may not be used by the customer in that strict order).

Emily draws a diagram of Rebel Insurance's core value stream, shown in Figure 11-1. Note that the wording of the services is written from Rebel Insurance's internal perspective, as opposed to the customer-centric language of the customer journey, which we will look at next.

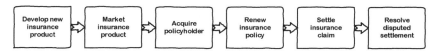

Figure 11-1 Rebel Insurance's core value stream

## The customer journey

Emily finds that the customer journey for Rebel Insurance is straightforward, like the value stream map but expressed from the customer perspective. Customers follow a simple lifecycle with their insurances – customers identify a need for insurance; discover insurers' product offerings; compare products; buy a policy; renew a policy; and make claims as necessary. If Rebel Insurance seems unfair in their assessment of a claim, the customer may need to dispute a claim settlement. Figure 11-2 shows Emily's depiction of this journey and the touchpoints with Rebel Insurance, where the customer gets information, interacts or transacts.

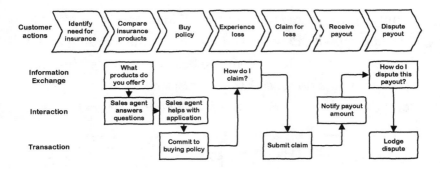

Figure 11-2 Rebel Insurance's journey map and key touchpoints

Looking at the touchpoints in the customer journey, Emily can see that there are three which appear to be transactions:

- Commit to buying policy
- Submit claim
- Lodge dispute.

These three touchpoints align with the transactional services that Rebel Insurance offers to its customers, as shown in the value stream map. That is, Rebel Insurance exists to enable customers to buy a suitable insurance policy, to submit a claim for an insured loss, and to dispute the company's settlement of a claim.

Emily could augment the customer journey map in various ways, by adding channels, business functions, and business capabilities. In this way, she can start to see how the internal structures and processing infrastructure align to the customer's point of view. Combining the value stream and the customer journey, Emily produces an initial view of the top tiers of the Rebel Insurance service blueprint, as shown in Figure 11-3.

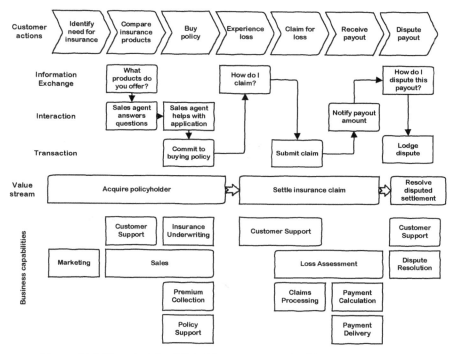

Figure 11-3 First sketch of Rebel Insurance service blueprint

## The business objects and data

Emily remembers that business objects are the 'things' that Rebel Insurance deals with; business objects (sometimes called 'entities' or 'data subjects') comprise data that describe those 'things'. Emily can now begin to discern, from the service blueprint, the business objects that are likely to be created or updated by Rebel Insurance's services. She needs to be aware of what these business objects are because this will help her to be clear about the purpose of each *transact* or *interact* touchpoint in the service journey. The *transact* touchpoints will create or update at least one type of business object that is part of the company's master data. For example, *Submit claim* will create a new Claim object.

---

**Business Object, Data Subject, Data Entity**

Commonly used labels for real world 'things' that a business stores data about.

---

Emily realizes that it is worth spending some time thinking about the business objects that are 'in the frame' for her business context, and about the relationships between the objects. She knows how important it is to carefully define each of these business objects, so that there is less confusion and ambiguity about what the terms mean. These steps will enable her to be clear about which master data each transaction might be creating or updating. Emily finds some obvious candidates for Rebel Insurance's business objects in the nouns used in the phrases that appear in Figure 11-3. These include:

- Policyholder
- Sales agent
- Policy
- Claim

- Payment
- Dispute.

She can also see from the service blueprint in Figure 11-3 that these business objects probably have relationships with each other – these relationships are expressed as a connecting verb. For example:

- Policyholder owns Policy
- Sales Agent sells Policy
- Payment settles Claim.

A diagram of the business objects and their relationships is somewhat easier to grasp than a list of relationships. So, Emily sketches out her thoughts about Rebel Insurance's data in the simple diagram shown in Figure 11-4.

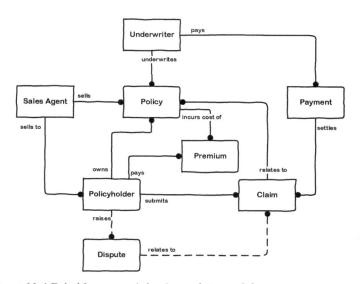

Figure 11-4 Rebel Insurance's business data model

This kind of diagram is called a **business data model**. Emily also compiles all of her definitions of the business objects in a Business Glossary.

Rebel Insurance probably has many more data objects that those shown here, but this level of detail is sufficient for the purpose of working through the design and specification of a transaction. If more details come to light later that are relevant to our objective, they can be added then. The diagrams shown in Figure 11-1 to Figure 11-4 can – and should – evolve as more discovery and design work is completed.

## Narrowing the focus to one transaction

So far, Emily has pieced together a fairly comprehensive idea of the business context of Rebel Insurance, the customer experience, and the kinds of data that Rebel Insurance works with. Now she will zoom in on one of the transaction touchpoints shown in the service blueprint – *Submit claim*.

Processing claims is the core operational process for Rebel Insurance – it consumes the bulk of the firm's work effort and involves a range of personnel with different skills. Insurers take care to assess each claim to ensure that the claim arises from a loss that is explicitly covered by the policy. In other words, claiming for losses against insurance policies generates a lot of transactions. Emily's goal in this case study is to redesign the *Submit claim* transaction, using the Transaction Pattern as the framework. She hopes to make the *Submit claim* transaction more efficient for the teams that process claims, and more effective for the customer, who wants their claim to be settled as quickly as possible.

## The business objects involved in the submit claim transaction

Because she is now focusing only on the *Submit claim* transaction, Emily can start to narrow her focus to the customer experience, business objects, and business functions that are involved specifically in this transaction.

She easily filters out the business objects that are not relevant to *Submit claim* by looking for the business object Claim in Figure 11-4 and finding the objects that are joined to it. These objects have a relationship to the Claim object which could be used or updated during the *Submit claim* transaction, so she needs to give them all some attention. By limiting her view in this way, she ends up with a smaller model showing only the business objects that she needs to consider when discussing *Submit claim* transactions, as shown in Figure 11-5.

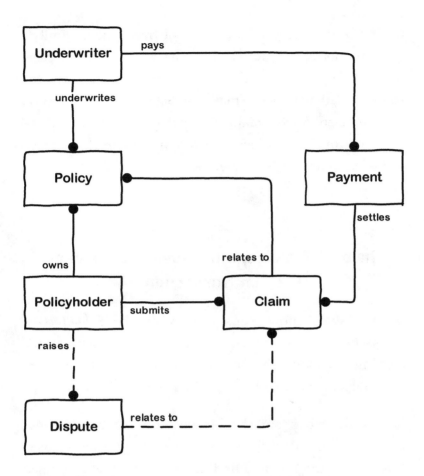

Figure 11-5 Rebel Insurance's business objects related to Claim

Emily revisits the service blueprint for Rebel Insurance (Figure 11-3) and notes that there is a *transaction* touchpoint after *Submit claim* called *Lodge dispute*. She realizes that these two transactions are separate because only a small proportion of all claims will be subject to a dispute; that is, they are made when the policyholder thinks that Rebel Insurance's assessment of their claim is unfair or mistaken. Therefore, she can remove the Dispute business object from Figure 11-5, because it will not be created or updated by a *Submit claim* transaction. Emily's resulting map of the relevant business objects is shown in Figure 11-6.

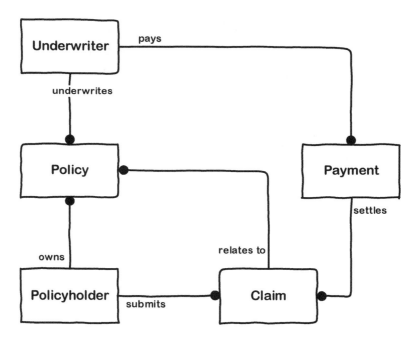

Figure 11-6 Business objects relevant to Submit claim transactions

The removal of Dispute from the scope of the business data model indicates that there is a clean finish to all *Submit claim* transactions, as they will be completed when a payment (or a rejection of the claim) is sent to the policyholder. If the policyholder is unhappy with the rejection or with the payment amount, they can commence

316 • EMILY'S REBELLION

a different – but related – transaction called *Lodge dispute*, and that is where the Dispute data is created.

This raises a vital point concerning how to distinguish different transactional services. It is relatively easy to get confused about the scope of your work and where your attention should be focused. We must be clear whether the scope of the project includes disputed claim settlements or not. If included in the scope, then Emily needs to ensure that the two transactions are kept separate in her design and (especially) in the requirements documentation. Emily becomes keenly aware that there are two transactions going on here. Allowing the two transactions to be jumbled together will complicate everything, not least the implementation of the transaction in systems.

Remember the request-and-response nature of the Transaction Pattern. The key question to ask is: "Is the customer making another request, and is there a separate decision that we make in response?" In the case of a disputed claim settlement, the answer to both questions is clearly "Yes". Also, consider whether the information that needs to be submitted by the customer is the same or different when lodging a dispute – a dispute must relate to a previously submitted claim, but the details of the claim do not need to be submitted again. Also, the policyholder may need to provide additional information to support their dispute. Therefore, *Submit claim* and *Lodge dispute* are separate transactions.

# The insurance claim business process

Emily knows that processing an insurance claim at Rebel Insurance not only involves several types of operators and assessors, but also some claims need the attention of senior claims assessors because of their complexity and/or high value. Simple or low-value claims may be processed and approved by junior staff, while complex or high-value claims will be investigated more thoroughly by a senior assessor and possibly approved by yet another person. In larger insurance companies, big claims teams deal with a large volume of claims for a wide range of policy types.

Emily sketches an outline of the processing steps. At Rebel Insurance, an insurance claim transaction is submitted online and processed through the following steps. Each step is carried out either by the insured person (or their representative) or by the insurer's front office and back office staff.

1.  The policyholder or a person representing the insured party (the 'insured') goes to Rebel Insurance's website, navigates to the place to make a claim, and identifies themselves and the insurance policy;

2.  They then enter the information required by the insurer, and may attach supporting evidence such as a photo of a damaged item, the original receipt

for the item's purchase, or a document that proves that an incident occurred (a police report or a death certificate, for example);

3. Rebel Insurance's website will validate that all the required information has been completed, and the website will invite the insured to review and submit the claim;

4. Inside the Rebel Insurance office, the attachments are checked for authenticity and relevance to the claim. A check will be made that the claim is valid under the policy.

5. If these checks pass, the claim is accepted for assessment and a letter is sent to the policyholder acknowledging receipt of the claim;

6. The claim is classified according to its policy type, complexity and potential value. The claim's classification is used to determine which teams will be involved in assessing it;

7. The Rebel Insurance assessor that is assigned to the claim conducts their assessment. This may be a straightforward process, or it may require further information from the insured, including a visit to view the extent of the loss incurred by the insured;

8. The assessor makes a decision to pay the claim or recommends such a decision to the claims

manager. In the latter case, the claims manager reviews the case and the assessor's recommendation and makes the decision. If the decision is to reject the claim, the next step is skipped.

9.   The amount of the payment is calculated, and the payment is made to the insured;

10.   A record of the decision and the payment amount is made and linked to the data about the customer's policy, for future reference;

11.   A letter is printed and sent to the insured to notify them of the decision and the payment amount (if any). The claim is now settled.

---

## Align the process to the Transaction Pattern

Emily notices that the basic pattern at play in the above sequence of activities conforms to the request-and-response Transaction Pattern. The submitter (the insured) submits a request (a claim). Rebel Insurance validates and assesses the claim, and either rejects the claim or agrees to pay an amount. The submitter is notified of Rebel Insurance's decision and, if applicable, receives the payment. Emily draws a diagram showing this alignment of the process steps with the Transaction Pattern, illustrated in Figure 11-7.

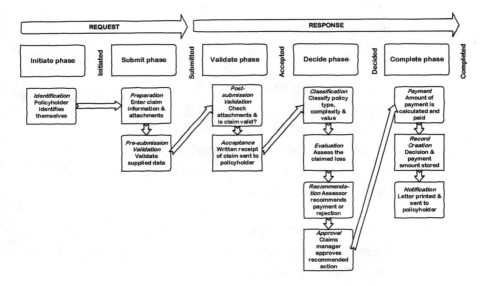

Figure 11-7 Submit claim processing steps aligned to Transaction Pattern

---

## Eliminate unnecessary business tasks

By comparing Figure 11-7 to the complete Transaction Pattern, Emily notices that some tasks described by the pattern are missing. The missing tasks are:

- Profiling
- Commencement Notification
- Acknowledgement
- Future Activity Scheduling.

Emily investigates each one of these tasks and makes sure that they are not required in the *Submit claim* transaction. For example, the Profiling task may be used if Rebel Insurance gives priority to claims received from high-value customers, or may flag the transaction as risky if the claimant is a known nuisance. The Acknowledgement task may be used, as an alternative to using the Acceptance task in the Validate phase, if Rebel Insurance wants to give immediate acknowledgement to the customer that the claim has been received.

In this example, a Classification task is required because Rebel Insurance's assessors are divided into junior and senior teams. The Senior Assessor team deals with complex and high-value claims. This means that each claim's Evaluation task must be classified as simple or complex, and low-value or high-value, so that it can be workflowed to a junior or a senior team of assessors. To further complicate matters, Rebel Insurance has a team of assessors for each policy type – life, vehicle, fire and general, etc. These factors mean that a received claim must be routed to a different team for assessment according to several business rules – complexity, potential value, and policy type. These rules may be implemented in a system, enabling automated routing of the Evaluation task to the work queue for the correct team. Rebel Insurance does not have this automation capability yet but would like to implement it soon. Currently, the complexity and value of each claim are classified by a human and they will manually assign the Evaluation task for the claim to the correct work queue.

Furthermore, high-value claims, once assessed, must be passed to a claims manager for approval. This facilitates separation of the duties between the senior assessor and the manager, enabling a check on the quality of the assessment and the recommended pay-out.

The separation of duties requires the Approval task to be workflowed to a task queue that is separate from the assessor queue. After performing the Evaluation task, the senior assessor may perform the Recommendation task to recommend a decision based on their assessment of the claim. When they mark the Recommendation task as 'done', the workflow will place a new task – Approval – on the claims manager's task queue. Since the senior assessor is not a member of the claims manager's queue, this mechanism prevents the senior assessor themselves from picking the Approval task.

Rebel Insurance has a policy that low-value claims can be approved by the same assessor that conducted the assessment of the claim; that is, they can approve their own work. This suggests that, in this case, the Evaluation task includes the Approval step. However, a well-designed workflow system will not combine the Approval task with the Evaluation task. This would 'hardwire' a rule that Rebel Insurance may want to alter in the future. For instance, keeping the Evaluation, Recommendation, and

Approval tasks separated allows a second assessor to approve the conclusion of the first assessor, perhaps after checking by a third assessor. Rebel Insurance might do this for quality and training purposes, or to introduce a separation of duties into the business process when on-boarding new staff (as above for high-value claims). They would not be able to do this – at least, not without making changes to the IT system – if the Evaluation, Recommendation, and Approval tasks were combined into one task for low-value claims.

Furthermore, since they want to be able to route approvals of high-value claims to a claims manager, the system must support separate Evaluation and Approval tasks. There is no additional cost to using the same mechanism for low-value claims.

In this example, we also see the Payment task in the Complete phase of the transaction. Recall that the tasks within the Complete phase cannot be stopped once the Approval task is finished. In the case of an insurance claim at Rebel Insurance, after the decision is made to pay the claim, the exact payment amount must be calculated, and an instruction sent to the accounts payable team to make the payment. This is the job of the Payment task.

Also, during the Complete phase, a letter is printed and sent to the insured party to notify them of Rebel Insurance's decision. This is the Notification task. There are standard payment letter and rejection letter templates.

The details of the claim and the payment amount are inserted into the template and the letter is generated.

---

## Holding a requirements workshop

Having sorted through how the work of the Claims Processing Department fits with the Transaction Pattern, Emily now wants to convene a workshop to discuss future requirements with her peers. She finds a date when the most experienced people are available for the whole day, then she chats with each of them individually to ensure they understand why it is important for them to attend. Emily also identifies three new hires in the department who seem to have fresh ideas and are open to doing their work differently.

Not feeling confident that she could facilitate the meeting as well as make good notes of the discussion, she invites an expert in the Transaction Pattern, Frank, to be the facilitator as well as an impartial observer.

Opening the workshop, Frank presents an overview of the Transaction Pattern and how it will help the team to design a better process. Then he leads the group through each phase of the Transaction Pattern, asking open questions at each step that stimulate the participants to share their knowledge and make observations about flaws in the current processes and systems.

Working through each task of the standard Transaction Pattern in turn, Frank writes notes on sheets of paper pinned to the wall of the room. From time to time, usually when the discussion revolves on a complex topic, Frank hands out colored sticky notepaper and invites the participants to write down data needs, business rules, the names of forms and letters, and the current issues that bother them, and to place them on the big sheets. Then Frank reads through all the sticky notes, aggregates similar notes, and moves them to where he thinks is the best place for them in the flow of the Transaction Pattern. Emily notices how this is a very efficient technique for extracting knowledge from people and stimulating group discussion about anything controversial.

The day progresses in this way until they reach the end of the Complete phase of the Transaction Pattern. Frank and Emily thank everyone for their active participation and they explain what will happen next. Emily takes photographs of all the sticky notes and wall sheets to distribute to the participants to encourage them to keep thinking about the issues. She gathers up all the sheets of paper to use as memory joggers when she sits down to compile the Transaction Requirements Document, which is the next step.

# Creating the transaction requirements document

Emily now has the task of transforming the output from the requirements workshop and any other discussions into a formal document which details the business requirements for the *Submit claim* transaction. Emily is best placed to write the document, as she is now thoroughly familiar with the Transaction Pattern and how her peers would like to see things change. Another person could do this job – like another subject matter expert, a business architect, or a business analyst – as long as they were closely involved in the requirements workshop.

Recalling the structure for the transaction requirements document that we proposed in Chapter 9, Emily organizes her document into four major parts. These four parts, and a few points about what Emily includes in each, are outlined below. These points are not exhaustive but are intended to illustrate the kind of content that the author should include and how the content should be expressed.

Part 1: Introduction
- In addition to the normal introductory comments that describe the purpose of, and the audience for, the document, Emily realizes that she needs to be clear about the scope of the document – i.e. what's in the document and what is not. Emily's scope statement states that the *Submit claim* transaction

includes the creation, validation, submission, assessment, approval and payment of claims for all policy types. The scope does not include disputed claim settlements, which are the subject of the *Lodge dispute* transaction.

Part 2: Transaction Overview

- To create her overview of the transaction, Emily assembles the various diagrams and descriptions outlined earlier in this chapter. These include: the customer journey map, the service blueprint, and the business data model. Also, Emily emphasizes the importance of the *Submit claim* transaction, since it is one of only two foundational pillars of Rebel Insurance, the other being selling insurance policies. The efficiency with which Rebel Insurance processes claims has a huge effect on the company's profitability.

- Emily also provides a brief section that states the things that must be true before a *Submit claim* transaction can commence (its pre-conditions) and the conditions that will exist when the transaction is finished (its post-conditions). These help readers of the document to be clear what triggers the transaction and what the result is.

Part 3: Transaction Requirements

- This part of the document specifies the detailed business requirements for each of the tasks throughout the Request and Response stages of the transaction. Each task is addressed in the order of the real-world sequence of operations. The contents of some key tasks are highlighted below.

- The Preparation task includes a list of the data that the claim submitter must complete. A sample from Emily's list follows:

| Data Element | Description |
|---|---|
| **Policyholder Name** <br> Mandatory | The name of the person who owns the relevant insurance Policy. |
| **Policy Number** <br> Mandatory | The number that uniquely identifies the Policy. |
| **Submitter Name** <br> Mandatory | The name of the person completing this claim if different to the Policyholder. |
| **Nature of Loss** <br> Mandatory | Description of what happened to cause the loss. |
| **Evidence** <br> Mandatory | One or more attachments – e.g. photograph, police report, purchase receipt, repair receipt. |

- The Post-submission Validation task specifies the rules that need to be checked before allowing the claim to be accepted for assessment. These include:

  o "Check the claimed loss is covered by the identified policy."

o "Check the contents of attachments are relevant to the claimed loss."

- The Classification task assigns the claim to the most appropriate work queue, so that it is handled by the correct team. It does this by assigning the Evaluation, Recommendation, and Approval tasks to the best queue, according to the business rules that we outlined earlier – i.e. the complexity of the claim, its potential value, and the policy type. Emily lists these task distribution rules in a table.

- The Evaluation task section lists the criteria that the claim assessor must consider, such as "Does the supplied evidence support the claim?" and "What portion of the loss is Rebel Insurance liable for?"

- The Record Creation task specifies the data that must be stored in master data, including the Claim data and its attachments, data about the Decision made by the Approver, and data about any settlement Payment that was made.

Part 4: Operational Requirements
- The final part includes the system performance requirements, such as "Availability – 99% during specified Hours of Operation." This part also includes any levers and switches that the business unit wants to be able to adjust without needing IT system changes, for example: "Add and remove

queues and queue allocation rules in the Classification task."

---

## Improving the transaction requirements document

With the first draft of the requirements document completed, Emily circulates her draft to the participants of the requirements workshop. She asks them to check that she has recorded the workshop discussion accurately. Then she asks them if they have had any other thoughts about things that were missed during the workshop or any new ideas.

Emily takes all this new input and edits her first draft, producing a second draft that is ready for broader distribution and review. After she has dealt with all the feedback from the broader group of stakeholders, Emily feels that the requirements document reflects a sound and much-improved way to process claims. The document is ready to be shown to the managers of her department. She proceeds by giving them a brief outline of how the proposed set of requirements based on the Transaction Pattern is structured and how it will change the way work is handled, making significant improvements in the department's efficiency and effectiveness. Emily then seeks endorsement from the team leads and, finally, formal approval of the document by the Claims Executive.

## Communicating the transaction requirements document

Emily has kept the key players of the IT and user experience teams and (especially) her business architect, abreast of the emerging requirements and has explained to them how the Transaction Pattern gives the requirements a logical structure. With approval of the Transaction Requirements Document behind her, Emily can now turn her full attention to communicating the revised requirements more fully to those teams – she can say to them authoritatively now: "this is what we want you to build."

## Three key points from this chapter

- The case study illustrates how to use the Transaction Pattern in Emily's situation.

- After understanding the business context of her transaction, Emily aligns the business process with the Transaction Pattern.

- Emily's requirements workshop gets all the key players aligned with the Transaction Pattern and allows Emily to rapidly discover more business requirements.

# CHAPTER 12

# Emily's Triumph

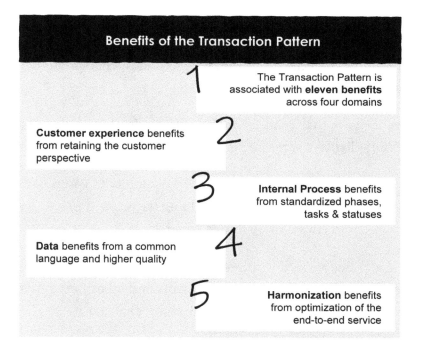

Emily is feeling triumphant. Her steps, tentative at first but growing bolder, are bearing fruit. These steps towards thinking differently about her business unit's processes and systems requirements have real benefits. Already her efforts have led to a simpler, streamlined workflow for the back-office processing of two transactional services. The quality of the data that the team collects has been improved because transaction data is not mixed up with the master data. Furthermore, her team is expressing requirements more clearly and communicating them more effectively to the IT system developers.

Emily is thrilled to hear that another team want to know about her techniques and have started to use them in their own project. There are signs that yet more teams will pick up the Transaction Pattern and want her to train them. Emily is becoming a leader of cultural change in her organization.

What is it that makes Emily a strong leader of change? Emily displays three key characteristics:

- She's rebellious – she shows an ability to confront the established ways of doing things, and is motivated to do things better;

- She's socially-entrenched – she's been involved in the project, and she represents and identifies with a whole group of people by being part of a professional community;

- She has a 'we can do anything' spirit – 'can do' people tend to lead change.

Emily moves to a new project where she again applies her new, rebellious thinking. The project team takes a bit of convincing at first, but Emily sees the light bulbs go on as her colleagues grasp how this method will help them.

Through her success, Emily leads the way for others to follow. She is beginning to see that, as more projects adopt the method, her ideas will diffuse throughout the organization over time.

Emily remembers the story of Rosa Parks, who in 1955 refused to give up her bus seat to a white person when the 'whites only' seats were full. This violated Alabama's segregation laws and Rosa was arrested. It seemed a small, rebellious act at the time, but because of her civil disobedience Rosa is remembered as the first lady of civil rights in the United States. It only takes one person to do something rebellious and change an entire organization.

Emily has watched other initiatives that started off strongly but then seemed to wither as time passed. The senior managers became nervous about whether the project would deliver the complete product, and trimmed scope from the project so that it delivered *something*. Management decisions like this inevitably mean that the intended benefits of the initiative are lost (or vastly diminished) and the 'return on investment' is small.

To prevent this happening to her initiative, Emily realizes that she needs to clearly articulate the benefits of adopting the Transaction Pattern and its associated techniques. She needs to show that each technique has its own benefits that will be realized when the technique is applied on its own. However, the benefits of using the individual techniques will be multiplied several times over when *all* the methods described in this book are adopted. Emily turns her mind to attaching benefits to each of the individual techniques, as well as how to show the cumulative effect of using the whole Transaction Pattern approach.

---

## A wide range of benefits

We have discussed several techniques and tools in this book that work together to deliver a range of benefits to the business. By using the Transaction Pattern, businesses can solve several problems that they commonly grapple with, including poor data quality and convoluted business processes.

There are immediate benefits that become evident when adopting any of these techniques separately. In this chapter, we discuss these benefits and how they arise from the Transaction Pattern techniques. As Emily has realized, however, when *all* the techniques are adopted, they work together to make a significant contribution to strategic objectives and outcomes, including increased customer value and increased organizational performance. We discuss these potential strategic outcomes in the final section of this chapter.

First, we summarize each technique and discuss the immediate benefits of using them. The techniques – and the benefits – fall into four areas, called 'domains':

- Internal Process domain
- Data domain
- Customer Experience domain
- Harmonization domain.

---

# Benefits in the internal process domain

The techniques related to the internal process perspective are the core of the Transaction Pattern. They include the following:

- Adopt the generalized pattern of stages, phases, and tasks for transaction processes

- Apply and reuse standardized shared work tasks to transaction processes

- Apply standardized transaction status codes across transaction processes.

These three techniques lead to substantial business benefits centered on decreasing costs and improving efficiency.

## Benefit #1: Decreased incidence of product variations

The framework provided by the Transaction Pattern encourages the design of processes that are agnostic to the product they handle. For example, the process for dealing with an insurance claim will be similar across all the company's insurance products. Likewise, the process for selling a car insurance policy will be like selling a travel insurance policy or a house insurance policy. The business rules that apply to each of these product types will, of course, be different but the business process can be identical when it is based on the Transaction Pattern.

This is a significant benefit because business processes, staff skills, data, and technology systems – that is, all aspects of the organization's business capabilities – become uniform across all product lines. The uniformity leads to increased business agility to respond quickly to market demands for new or different products, and considerably reduced cost of doing so.

## Benefit #2: Common process vocabulary across organization

This benefit derives from using the terminology of the Transaction Pattern, as shown again in Figure 12-1. By adopting the terminology for the phases, tasks, and transaction statuses prescribed by the Transaction Pattern, everyone will have a shared understanding of the process vocabulary. This means that the process terms will be used consistently and unambiguously, leading to faster, more effective discussions about business requirements and improvements.

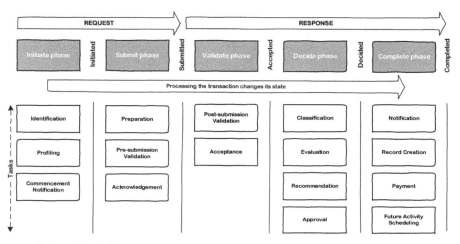

Figure 12-1 The Transaction Pattern

## Benefit #3: Increased flexibility to compose processes from standard components

The Transaction Pattern partitions a business process into tasks, each of which has a specific and contained function. For example, Identification does nothing more than identify the submitter. The Preparation task is where the submitter provides the required information, and that's all. Validation of the information prepared by the submitter belongs in a separate activity.

By leveraging this aspect of the Transaction Pattern, you can investigate the possible inefficiencies in the current business process. You can recognize when, say, a validation check is currently performed in an inefficient or ineffective place such as after some of the evaluation work has commenced. A validation activity performed here will interrupt the work of evaluating the request. The Transaction Pattern will guide you towards moving the validation check to the Post-submission or Pre-submission Validation tasks, along with all other validation rules.

The Transaction Pattern also helps with confining notifications sent to the customer to pre-defined points in the journey where there is a specific need for communication between the business and customer. These include acknowledging the receipt of a request from the customer, notifying the customer of the business's response to the request, and notifying them of a new transaction that the business is initiating. The pattern will ensure that a notification is not inserted randomly within another task, making the processing sequence tighter and more efficient.

Rather than serving to constrain new or unusual process designs, this aspect of the Transaction Pattern brings flexibility to process design. For one thing, the sequencing of tasks is not fixed – there are circumstances, such as when a transaction is case-like (as described in Chapter 3), when the order of tasks needs to be varied from the standard pattern. This altered sequencing can still be achieved without compromising the purpose of each task. Also, several sub-tasks may be prescribed within a task – there is no constraint on what work is performed within a task, provided all sub-tasks work towards the purpose of the task.

## Benefit #4: Increased completeness and accuracy of operational reports

Standardization also occurs by constraining the status codes of transactions to a very limited number. The status codes are the same for all types of transactions. We discussed in Chapter 3 how the Transaction Pattern comprises a sequence of phases of work performed by the customer and the business operations. When each phase is completed, the status of the transaction changes. A great benefit of this uniformity of statuses is that it enables straight-forward reporting of the status of all types of transactions.

Operational managers can easily obtain a list of all the transactions that are in progress and filter the list to suit their management needs. Using the list of active transactions, managers can analyze that data to look for operational issues. For example, one use might be to find all the transactions across all services, which have held a status of Submitted for more than a week – this could indicate a problem area that is at risk of missing the service level targets.

Standardized transaction statuses also mean that customers – if you give them the tools, such as self-service portals and mobile apps – can readily help themselves to up-to-date information about the progress of their transactions, both current and historical. The list of transactions relevant to a customer can be extracted from the transaction database, projected to digital channels, and easily filtered and sorted by the user. This delivers self-service status reporting across all transactional services. When transaction data is specific to a transaction type and stored in separate tables, or when transaction status codes are not standardized, status reporting requires the collation of entries from multiple database tables. This is much costlier to implement and maintain and will deliver a worse customer experience than the centralized approach offered by the Transaction Pattern.

Managers of a firm's daily operations need dashboards that present simple information in an easy-to-access form. The instruments on the management dashboard are not unlike the instruments on a car's dashboard. Just as a driver needs a speedometer to drive the car safely, so an operations manager needs a workload meter, a workforce meter, a throughput meter, a 'stuck tasks' meter, a service level meter, and so on. The operations manager cannot 'drive' the operation at its best performance without these meters. They enable a manager to see quickly whether their teams are meeting service levels, whether they have enough people to get the work done, and whether there are any blockages in their processes. All of this information helps a manager to do their job effectively and address issues quickly.

This benefit is amplified many times by using the same set of statuses across all the business's types of transactions. The resulting management reports can present status information in real-time, allowing managers to quickly become aware of and act on operational problems. In fact, dashboards displaying real-time information about the state of the business's operations are <u>only</u> practical when using standardized transaction statuses across all processes. Such dashboards are fiendishly difficult when there is no uniformity in statuses; reports usually need to be adjusted manually to enable comparison across different transaction types. The benefits in the internal process domain from using the techniques are illustrated in Figure 12-2.

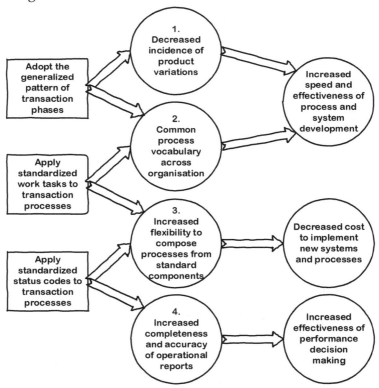

Figure 12-2 Benefits in the Internal Process domain

Taking these immediate benefits a step further, Emily realizes that by using the Transaction Pattern as the framework for designing business processes, her organization will be able to develop systems and process improvements faster, cheaper, and with flexibility by assembling from these standard components. Better accuracy in operational reports will lead to better decision making in managing operations.

---

# Benefits in the data domain

The data-related techniques Emily has learned include the following:

- Develop a business glossary
- Model and manage master data
- Generalize transaction data.

These techniques lead to business benefits centered on increased data quality.

### Benefit #5: A shared understanding of business terms

A business glossary standardizes the organization's terminology. It is a fundamental requirement of making any improvement in the quality of the data held by the organization. By defining terms precisely and unambiguously, the organization cuts through the problem of two or more business silos using a common term that means something different to each of them. Even when the difference in meaning is slight, it can manifest in negative ways such as misunderstanding between business units, ineffective collaboration when they need to work together, and, consequently, behavioral conflict.

The precise definition of the organization's terminology leads to structuring the data more logically so that data about each thing is kept together and not mixed with data about other things. Consequently, the fields (on screens and forms) for capturing data about different things will be separated and clearly distinguished by accurate field labeling and explanatory text.

## Benefit #6: Increased data quality

While a transaction to update a person's address is in progress, would you want other transactions for the same customer to read the new address or the old one? Obviously, we don't want to send correspondence to an old address when the customer has recently told us they have moved. However, correspondence should not be generated for the new address before the address has been validated as correct and the update confirmed. While this example is somewhat unrealistic because with modern systems the address could be validated and written to the database in milliseconds, it illustrates the point that sound controls are necessary when updating a master data record.

The transaction data, when implemented in IT systems, keeps in-progress data updates away from other processes that might happen at the same time. It does this by keeping newly updated 'candidate' data separate from the confirmed master data until the business transaction that is causing the update has reached a Completed state. This separation mandates good control over data updates, preventing the use of candidate data until it has been confirmed and written to the master data tables. The latter step occurs, you will recall, in the Record Creation task of the Complete phase of the Transaction Pattern.

At first glance it may seem that this level of control is a bad thing because it imposes restrictions on business operations. However, these restrictions can save the business from itself at times. The control prevents, say, an airline selling my seat on a flight before I have paid the cancellation fee for my booking. If I don't want to pay it, the cancellation will not be confirmed – I might change my mind and travel anyway. The control also prevents a government agency from paying a benefit into a new bank account before they have exercised the verification to ensure that the new account belongs to the beneficiary and not to a fraudster.

The Transaction Pattern, when implemented in a system, imposes these kinds of controls to master data updating.

Even when not implemented in systems, the pattern encourages discussion during the requirements specification about what controls on the use of master data records are necessary when a transaction is underway.

The Transaction Pattern provides a sound structure for controlling updates to master data during business operations, thereby lifting the quality of master data so that it is fit for purpose in other transactions and reports.

## Benefit #7: Increased management of data

The Transaction Pattern, when implemented in the information systems of a business, centralizes the data created by its transactions with customers. Every transaction deposits data into the databases. As we explored in Chapter 2, transactions create and update master data, such as a new customer record or a new bank account record. But transactions also create data about themselves – this is called 'transaction data'.

The business uses the transaction data to manage its day-to-day operations. Transaction data keeps track of what has happened to a transaction in the business process – who submitted it, what tasks have been done on it, who did the work, when they did it, what its current state is in the workflow.

When the Transaction Pattern is built into systems, your transaction data is centralized and standardized across all types of transactions. There is a saving in doing this, as it reduces complexity in the database, thus reducing the cost of the software that creates and retrieves transaction data.

Because implementing the Transaction Pattern stores transaction data in one place for all types of transactions, it also provides a central store of all the approval decisions made for every transaction. This means that a business approval given at any time in the past can be readily retrieved, along with the context and evidence surrounding that decision.

The benefits from using the techniques in the data domain are illustrated in Figure 12-3.

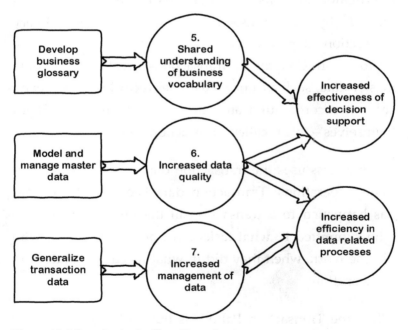

Figure 12-3 Benefits in the Data Domain

Emily now understands how the data domain techniques – using a business glossary, managing master data, and generalizing transaction data – give rise to immediate benefits in improved data quality, better understanding of the contents of data, and more-conscious management of master data and transaction data. By leveraging these benefits, Emily's business can realize further benefits including making better business decisions (because management information has higher quality) and increased efficiency in processes required for managing the organization's data.

## Benefits in the customer experience domain

There are two techniques related to Customer Experience that really helped Emily's understanding:

- Employ the Service Design approach
- Design standardized customer interactions, touchpoints, and channels.

These techniques lead to business benefits centered on creating a stronger value proposition for customers; they create a smoother, more customer-centered experience.

## Benefit #8: Increased alignment of business model to customer perspective

The several techniques of the Service Design approach ensure that the perspective of the customer is strongly present during the design of a transactional service. When Service Design techniques are used in combination with the Transaction Pattern, the customer perspective is retained during the specification of business requirements for system implementation and business process re-engineering.

## Benefit #9: Interaction design is driven by customer experience

If the ways in which the business and the customer interact are standardized, then interaction recording, notifications, and correspondence will always occur using the same tools. This avoids the need to discover, design, and implement interaction tools and methods for every type of transaction. The design of these standardized interactions should be derived from the desired customer experience, which in turn is based on 'knowing the customer' through user research and other Service Design techniques.

The benefit to customer experience is that they receive consistent interactions whenever they make contact with the business; customers learn to know what to expect when they need to interact and their frustrations with the previous ways of interacting diminish.

Emily sketches out the techniques in the customer experience domain and the immediate benefits of using them, shown in Figure 12-4. By using the Service Design approach and standardizing customer interactions across all transactional services, a business can realize immediate benefits by stronger awareness of, and alignment with, how customers actually experience the service. Emily believes these two benefits work together to build a stronger value proposition, suggesting that customers will be more likely to use the organization's services.

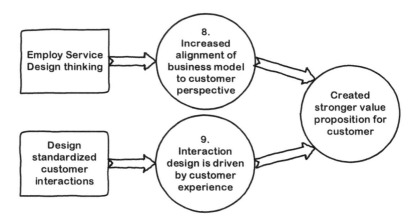

Figure 12-4 Benefits in the Customer Experience domain

## Benefits in the harmonization domain

Finally, two techniques harmonize the customer journey with the internal process journey. These are the following:

- Align Service Blueprints with the Transaction Pattern
- Employ the Transaction Pattern to structure requirements specifications.

These techniques lead to business benefits centered on increased optimization of the end-to-end service pathway.

## Benefit #10: Aligned external and internal process designs

As we saw in our discussion of the Service Design approach in Chapter 4, Service Design emphasizes the customer perspective and their experience of services. In contrast, the Transaction Pattern is primarily concerned with the internal processing tasks of the business, but also includes the tasks performed by the customer. The pattern serves to clearly link the customer journey and the internal process journey at a deeper level of detail than Service Design alone can achieve.

In Chapter 1 we discussed that there are not one, but two journeys that interact at several touchpoints – the customer journey and the internal process journey. When a touchpoint involves the customer transacting with the business, a transaction occurs, as shown in Figure 12-5.

The Transaction Pattern links the internal journey with the customer journey by defining and sequencing the activities that both stakeholders – the customer and the business –

perform during a transaction. The pattern lays out a framework for specifying these activities in a consistent manner for all transactional services.

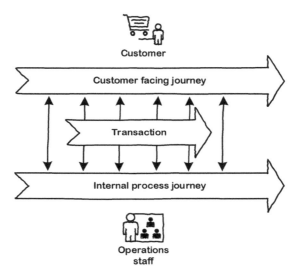

Figure 12-5 Transactions occur at defined touchpoints within journeys

In this way, using the Transaction Pattern complements the products created by the service design approach, including the customer journey and the service blueprint. Together, these tools ensure that the customer perspective is retained in the specification and implementation of the internal process journey.

## Benefit #11: Increased effectiveness of communication with system builders

The Transaction Pattern provides a framework used for structuring transaction requirements workshops. We discussed how to structure and manage requirements workshops using this framework in Chapter 9. The benefit of this approach to running requirements workshops is that it centers the discussion on the customer perspective and the operational needs of the business. Requirements discovery workshops conducted by IT are usually centered on the computer system screens, thereby pushing customer and operational needs to the background.

The Transaction Pattern improves your ability to communicate effectively with your IT colleagues when system builds or enhancements are needed. The requirements specification document that we introduced in Chapter 9 contains most of the information that the IT team should require to commence system design work. There should be very limited need for the IT team to discover further requirements and engage in prolonged consultation with business teams on their requirements.

The IT team may resist this approach, as it is not what they are used to. IT commonly prefers to engage with business experts, individually and through lengthy workshops, to find out 'what the business really wants'. IT will be uncomfortable with the new approach, at least at first. Be strong and try to push through this resistance.

It is important to explain to your IT colleagues that the requirements specification based on the Transaction Pattern does not specify screen layouts and other IT-specific domains. A requirements specification, based on the framework of the Transaction Pattern, frames the operational needs of the business within the context of the purpose of the transactional service and the desired customer experience. Equipped with this knowledge, IT designers and system analysts can concentrate their work on IT-related design matters, using tools such as screen design, IT solution architecture, and user story definition.

The Transaction Pattern provides you with a framework for briefing the IT team on the business's requirements. Resist the temptation to simply send the requirements document 'over the wall' to your IT project manager or another contact in the IT team. Invite the team to a briefing at which you walk through the requirements. At the briefing, begin with an outline of the whole transactional service and where it fits in the broader business context. Then work your way through the Transaction Pattern step-by-step, outlining the processing and data requirements for each task.

The benefits from using the techniques in the harmonization domain are illustrated in Figure 12-6.

To summarize the benefits in this domain, harmonizing the internal process journey with the customer journey and structuring the requirements specification around the Transaction Pattern will optimize the end-to-end service pathway and increase the organization's speed of development. Emily wonders, however, whether these two immediate benefits may also flow into other benefits in the other domains that we have already discussed. For example, would better optimization of the end-to-end service pathway contribute to building an improved value proposition or perhaps increased process efficiency?

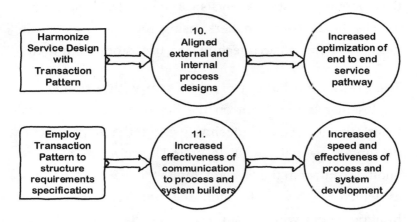

Figure 12-6 Benefits in the Harmonization Domain

We explore Emily's thoughts further in the final section, in which we discuss the contributions that all of the above benefits make towards the achievement of strategic outcomes.

## The direct benefits ultimately contribute to strategic outcomes

The eleven benefits across the four domains described above are the immediate benefits of using the Transaction Pattern and its associated techniques. As we saw in the previous sections and the diagrams showing the 'flow' of benefits, the immediate benefits give rise to more significant benefits – these are known as 'intermediate benefits'. Intermediate benefits, in turn, contribute to genuine and sustained improvements in the operations of the organization. These strategic outcomes relate to two areas:

- improving effectiveness (by delivering better value to customers), and
- improving efficiency (by delivering increased business performance).

Figure 12-7 illustrates how the intermediate benefits in the Customer Experience, Harmonization, Internal Process, and Data domains flow towards the achievement of strategic outcomes.

Emily notices that Figure 12-7 shows benefits from adopting the techniques in the customer experience domain contribute to the strategic objective of increased customer value, but not at all to the objective of increased business performance. This demonstrates that we cannot expect to derive efficiencies by focusing solely on improving our customers' experience. We must instead place greater emphasis on adopting the techniques in the internal process domain and the data domain. The converse also applies: we cannot deliver more customer value by making improvements only in the internal process or data domains.

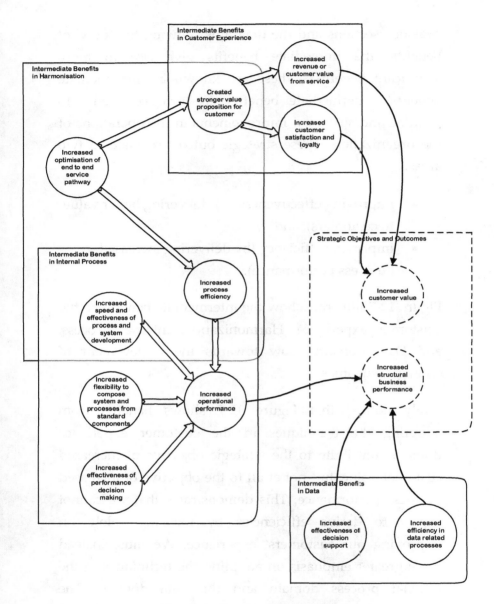

Figure 12-7 Intermediate Benefits contribute to Strategic Outcomes

Typically, businesses strive to make improvements in both strategic outcomes (among others, depending on the business strategy). Therefore, all the techniques presented in this book, which are centered on the Transaction Pattern, will work together to deliver a significant contribution to both improved customer value and increased business performance.

The benefits we have discussed in this chapter demonstrate precisely why Emily has taken up the revolutionary flag and instigated a rebellion. As you take these new tools back to your own workplace, we hope you also find the Transaction Pattern is a tool to assist in the constant search for business improvement and innovation, and more successful delivery of your business's priorities and projects.

---

## Three key points from this chapter

- Immediate benefits can be gained from using any of the techniques described in this book.

- Benefits are multiplied by using the Transaction Pattern and all its associated techniques.

- Applying the Transaction Pattern to your business will ultimately help with achieving strategic outcomes, like increased customer value and increased business performance.

---

# Further reading

*Benefits Realisation Management Framework.* (2015) State of New South Wales. Retrieved from: https://bit.ly/2QzJFog.

Harries, Sarah and Peter Harrison (2009). "IT Value Special Compilation"; ISACA Journal; Retrieved from: https://bit.ly/2DVFAni.

Jenner, Steve. (2014) "Managing Benefits – Second Edition". The Stationery Office.

Thorp, John. (2007). "The Information Paradox: Realizing the Business Benefits of Information Technology". Fujitsu Consulting. Retrieved from: https://bit.ly/2PaSFLC.

# BIBLIOGRAPHY

Ambler, Scott, (2018) "Data Modelling 101" Retrieved from: https://bit.ly/2KNUVYG.

*Benefits Realisation Management Framework.* (2015) State of New South Wales. Retrieved from: https://bit.ly/2QzJFog.

Business Architecture Guild®. (2018) "The Business Architecture Quick Guide: A Brief Guide for Gamechangers" Meghan-Kiffer Press.

Carey, Craig. (2015) "The Origin of Writing". Retrieved from: https://bit.ly/2Pdxetn (includes photos of tokens, bulla, tablets and cuneiform).

Clark, Mike, Whynde Kuehn, Chalon Mullins, Eric Spellman. (2016) "Business Architecture and the Customer Experience: A Comprehensive Approach for Turning Customer Needs into Action". Business Architecture Guild®. Retrieved from: https://bit.ly/2FPIFrW.

Davies, Lyn. (2006) "A is for Ox – A short history of the alphabet". Folio Society.

Harries, Sarah and Peter Harrison (2009). "IT Value Special Compilation"; ISACA Journal; Retrieved from: https://bit.ly/2DVFAni.

Hoberman, Burbank, and Bradley. (2009) "Data Modeling for the Business – A handbook for aligning the business with IT using high-level data models". Technics Publications.

Jenner, Steve. (2014) "Managing Benefits – Second Edition". The Stationery Office.

Mager, Birgit. (2013) "Introduction to Service Design - What is Service Design?" Service Design Network. Retrieved from: https://youtu.be/f5oP_RlU91g.

Potts, Chris (2010a) "RecrEAtion". Technics Publications.

--------------- (2010b) "Measuring the Architectural Performance of an Enterprise: Using Structural Performance Ratios to Guide Investments in Enterprise Architecture". Retrieved from: https://bit.ly/2KKgh9f.

Reason, Ben; Løvlie, Lavrans and Flu, Melvin Brand. (2016) "Service Design for Business"; Wiley.

Simsion, Graeme & Graham Witt. (2006) "Data Modeling Essentials", 3rd Edition. Morgan Kaufmann.

Thorp, John. (2007). "The Information Paradox: Realizing the Business Benefits of Information Technology". Fujitsu Consulting. Retrieved from: https://bit.ly/2PaSFLC.

Ulrich, William M. and Whynde, Kuehn. (2015) "Business Architecture: Dispelling Ten Common Myths". Business Architecture Guild. Retrieved from: https://bit.ly/2E9weWa.

*Service Blueprint* in Wikipedia. Retrieved on 18th September, 2018 from https://bit.ly/2Q5U4IB.

*A key to service innovation: Services blueprinting*; W.P. Carey School of Business, Arizona State University. Retrieved on 19th September, 2018 from https://bit.ly/2BKSrr3.

# Index

Acceptance task, 189, 263, 274, 321

Acknowledgement task, 211, 262, 274, 321

Agile development, 19, 122, 288–91

Approval task, 178, 179, 201, 208–9, 225–26, 264, 274, 322

Architecture
Buildings, 26, 137–41
Business, 29, 122, 137–42, 148–60
System, 21, 210, 283

Authentication, 217, 216–22

Benefits
in Customer Experience, 337, 351, 357
in Data Management, 337, 357
in Harmonization, 337, 351, 355
in Internal Processes, 336, 337, 343, 357

Beta testing, 20

Bulla, 35

Business capabilities, 29, 144

Business Context, 272

Business Data Model, 192, 194, 195, 272, 311, 312, 315, 327

Business functions, 30, 106, 116, 157, 272, 280, 308, 312, 313

Business Levers, 279

Business objects, 309–16, 314, See data subjects

Business process, 8, 24, 30, 41, 64, 74, 101, 141, 150, 165, 166, 187, 254, 269, 304, 306, 317, 323

Business requirements, 5, 11, 25, 129, 212, 213, 216, 230, 241, 244, 255, 268, 273, 275, 283

Business service, 30

Classification task, 177, 264, 274, 321

Commencement Notification task, 260, 274

Complete Phase, 179, 180, 181

Cuneiform, 37

Customer journey, 17, 23, 30, 43, 83, 106, 114, 118, 119, 124, 125, 145, 149, 158, 259, 269, 272, 304, 307

Dashboard, 75, 342
Data
    Audit Data, 49, 51, 58
    Master Data, 48, 51, 57,
        60, 190
    Metadata, 51, 58, 244,
        247
    Reference Data, 51, 58,
        74, 275, 279
    Structure Data, 51, 58
    Transaction Data, 49, 51,
        57, 62, 63, 65
Data concepts. See data
    subjects
Data entity, 310
Data model, 31
Data processing, 40, 49
Data subjects, 41, 46, 159,
    309, 310
Decide phase, 177–79
Digitization, 13, 16, 91
Evaluation task, 178, 185,
    209, 264, 265, 274, 321
Future Activity
    Scheduling task, 182,
        227, 267
Glossary
    Business, 30, 45, 297,
        312, 344
    Emily's, 29
Identification task, 216,
    217, 260
Implementing the
    Transaction Pattern,
    300–302

Information service, 30, 31
Initiate phase, 170, 259, 274
Interaction, 31, 230, 233,
    234, 237, 238, 251
Interaction Recording, 233,
    234, 239, 251
Notification task, 216, 224,
    266, 323
Nouns, 36, 53, 156, 192, 310
Operational management,
    101, 195, 279
Operational requirements,
    270, 279
Operational throughput,
    49
Organizational Change
    Management, 293, 294
Payment task, 181, 224,
    225, 267, 274, 323
Post-submission
    Validation task, 189,
    263, 274
Preparation task, 225, 261,
    274
Pre-submission Validation
    task, 262, 274, 340
Profiling task, 260, 321
Queue, 31, 186, 187, 189,
    202, 207, 212, 226, 279,
    321
Rebus Principle, 38
Recommendation task,
    178, 264, 274, 322
Record Creation task, 266,
    274, 329, 346

Request for more information, 207, 248

Request stage, 77, 87, 90, 170–76, 254

Response stage, 77, 90, 176–82

Responsible party (of transaction), 201

Service blueprint, 31, 118, 149, 304

Service Design, 31, 123, 158, 230, 258

Subject (of transaction), 171, 201

Subject matter expert, 270, 304, 326

Submit phase, 173

Submitter, 171, 189, 201, 207, 221, 260, 319

Task, 31, 98, 183, 194, 202, 247, 273

Task Status, 183, 194

Touchpoint, 83, 106, 116, 124, 239, 310

Transaction, 31, 76–82

Transaction complexity, 95–103

Transaction Pattern, 5, 11, 73–103, 108, 119, 122, 167–70

Transaction requirements, 123, 189, 268, 280, 281, 326, 330, 331

Transaction status, 88, 102, 337, 341, 342

Transactional service, 25, 30, 32, 58, 78, 119, 161, 200, 213, 222, 228, 308, 316

Users, 185, 195, 202

Validate phase, 101, 176, 262, 274, 321

Value stream, 32, 145–49, 259, 304, 306

Verbs, 36–39, 127, 166

Waterfall development, 19, 296

Workflow, 32, 96, 107, 122, 123, 156, 182-189, 195, 197, 207, 211, 254, 255, 264, 268, 270, 299, 304, 322, 333, 347

Workshop, requirements, 254–68, 284, 299, 324, 354

www.ingramcontent.com/pod-product-compliance
Lightning Source LLC
Chambersburg PA
CBHW071232050326
40690CB00011B/2077

* 9 7 8 1 6 3 4 6 2 4 6 1 9 *